Gary —

Creativity is

free!

(signature)

Praise for *Disney U*

"When I first arrived at The Walt Disney Company, I was surprised to find I had to go back to school—at Disney University! There, I learned the fundamentals of guest service that consistently gave Disney a tremendous advantage in the marketplace. Now, anyone can know these secrets of success, thanks to Doug Lipp's informative book. No matter what your business, the lessons taught at Disney University will prove invaluable."

Michael Eisner, former CEO and Chairman of The Walt Disney Company

"Doug Lipp shares terrific stories about Disney that underscore the importance of creating an organizational culture with an unwavering dedication to superlative service and exceptional quality, both for employees and customers. He then takes it a step further by explaining how to bring these values to life for your organization."

Christine A. Morena, Executive Vice President of
Human Resources, Saks Incorporated

"*Disney U* does a masterful job of detailing how Disney has built a brand that transcends generations and cultures. Doug Lipp has created much more than the standard "how to" business book. *Disney U* provides numerous compelling, behind-the-scenes stories that bring to life Walt Disney's timeless values of employee development, attention to detail, and the relentless pursuit of quality. I highly recommend *Disney U* to anyone interested in building an enduring market presence and brand."

Stephen Cannon, President and Chief Executive Officer,
Mercedes-Benz USA

"Van France and the Disney University team embody a famous Walt Disney quote, "The best is never the best." Doug Lipp's riveting narratives reveal how Van and other Disney visionaries set the stage for a world-class organization by skillfully balancing both 'people' and 'technology.'"

Debi Aubee, Vice President of Sales, Bose Corporation

"Walt Disney and Van France were masters at creating employee education that was entertaining, memorable, and effective. Although I've read many books about Disney, I'd never heard about Van France and his role in founding the iconic Disney University. Every leader should have the equivalent of a Van France at his or her side. Thanks to Doug Lipp, we can now tap into the brilliance of a man who helped Walt create The Happiest Place on Earth."

David Overton, Founder and Chief Executive Officer,
The Cheesecake Factory

"Disney U should be required reading for anyone that deals with the public!"
Marty Sklar, retired Vice Chairman, Walt Disney Imagineering

"A culture of providing exceptional leadership, teamwork and customer service has long been attributed to Disney, yet very few know about the role the Disney University plays in creating extraordinary outcomes. How does the Disney University create such enthusiastic, loyal, and customer-centered employees, year after year? Now, for the first time, Doug Lipp takes us on a journey backstage to answer this pivotal question. Doug's compelling prose provides illustrative examples of how Disney visionaries, including Walt Disney and Van France, overcame daunting challenges using creativity, tenacity, and a dogged insistence on staying true to a crystal-clear set of values. In so doing, he provides a roadmap for other organizations seeking to excel."

John G. Veres III, PhD, Chancellor, Auburn University at Montgomery

"Leaders, whether at the helm of a ship or an organization, set the tone for engaging the hearts and minds of employees. In *Disney U*, Doug Lipp shares how Disney has created a high-performance culture where everyone takes ownership and responsibility. The numerous examples detailing the secrets behind the decades of success of the Disney University serve as a leadership blueprint, applicable in any organization."

Captain D. Michael Abrashoff (Ret.), former Commander, *USS Benfold*, author, *It's Your Ship: Management Techniques from the Best Damn Ship in the Navy*

"The lessons Doug Lipp shares in *Disney U* about how and why Disney excels are proof that an organization which knows more and cares more about its employees, will do so with its customers . . . and be the winner every time!"

Robert B. Engel, President and Chief Executive Officer, CoBank

"How many of us have experienced the magic of a good show, performed by courteous cast members, at The Happiest Place on Earth? In *Disney U*, Doug Lipp articulates the method behind the magic and offers a clear view of how any organization can create a culture where its guests will always want to return. Simple, understandable and widely applicable, Disney U captures the essence of what perpetuates Disney's success and can certainly add to yours."

Ryan C. Beasley, Vice President, Agencies, Kansas City Life Insurance Company

"Doug creates a masterpiece in *Disney U* through sharing the formation of the values and virtues of Disney University and the Disney culture. Doug Lipp's entertaining and informative analysis of the secrets of the Disney University create the perfect learning tool for any organization or leader."

Doug Stark, President and CEO, Farm Credit Services of America

"I should never have started *Disney U* so close to bedtime—I stayed up half the night reading it! I couldn't put it down; . . . spellbinding insights articulately presented. One of the best business books I've ever read."

Jeffrey L. Rupp, President, FlashPoint Productions

DISNEY U

How the Disney University Develops the World's Most Engaged, Loyal, and Customer-Centric Employees

DOUG LIPP

New York   Chicago   San Francisco   Lisbon   London   Madrid   Mexico City
Milan   New Delhi   San Juan   Seoul   Singapore   Sydney   Toronto

6 7 8 9 0 DOC/DOC 1 8 7 6 5

ISBN: 978-0-07-180807-1
MHID: 0-07-180807-8

e-ISBN: 978-0-07-180808-8
e-MHID: 0-07-180808-6

Doug Lipp is not affiliated with, and is not a representative of The Walt Disney Company.

Academy Award® and Oscar® are registered trademarks of the American Academy of Motion Pictures Arts and Sciences. Tony Awards® is a registered trademark of the American Theatre Wing, Inc. Grammy Awards® is a registered trademark of the National Academy of Recording Arts & Sciences, Inc.

McGraw-Hill books are available at special quantity discounts to use as premiums and sales promotions, or for use in corporate training programs. To contact a representative, please e-mail us at bulksales@mcgraw-hill.com.

Library of Congress Cataloging-in-Publication Data
Lipp, Doug.
    Disney U : how Disney University develops the world's most engaged, loyal, and customer-centric employees / by Doug Lipp. — 1 Edition.
        pages cm
    ISBN-13: 978-0-07-180807-1 (alk. paper)
    ISBN-10: 0-07-180807-8 (alk. paper)
    1. Customer relations—Management. 2. Employee motivation. 3. Employees—Training of. 4. Success in business. 5. Disney University. I. Title.
    HF5415.5L5657 2013
    658.3'124—dc23   2013002473

To Walt and Van

CONTENTS

Foreword

Walt Disney and Van France are American originals.

Due to their ground-breaking efforts, the world is a much better place for all of us. Many thousands of pages in books and countless hours in documentaries and films have analyzed Walt's inimitable combination of creativity, compassion, and his uncompromising quality standards. The lessons Walt taught me and many others could fill a library.

However, virtually nothing has been written about my mentor, Van France, and his role as the founder of the Disney University. I was fresh out of the Army and working at Disneyland when, during a chance meeting with Walt Disney, he suggested I talk with Van about some ideas I had about training at Disneyland. Walt said to me, "There's a guy over in Administration named Van France who you might like to meet. Van is starting something called the University of Disneyland. If you're interested in doing training, go meet Van and tell him Walt sent you."

Van ultimately asked me and several others to help him start what became the Disney University. Our relationship spanned over 30 years, and during that time Van became a trusted advisor and dear friend.

Van was a gifted educator and coach. His uncanny ability to effectively package and convey information was due to his ability to listen and earn trust, vital prerequisites for any leader. He really listened! Van didn't always agree with what he heard and was definitely not a pushover (qualities to which many Disney executives can attest). Yet, aside from Walt Disney, I can't think of anyone more skilled at connecting with cast members, at every level of the organization.

Van wore his heart on his sleeve and provided honest feedback. He was equally comfortable challenging everything, from the usefulness of the longest-standing policies to the leadership approaches of the most powerful. Van had courage.

I kept Van in mind throughout the Tokyo Disney Resort and Disneyland Paris Resort projects. Years earlier, he taught me that one person can't do it all. He taught me to think creatively and to delegate. He wasn't a micromanager, but he held people responsible for getting things done.

Walt Disney's and Van France's lessons inspired me and countless Disney cast members around the world. Through *Disney U*, it is my sincere hope that these lessons will take their rightful place on the global stage.

—Jim Cora, retired chairman, Disneyland International

Acknowledgments and Cast Credits

Disney U is in your hands thanks to the unwavering support and trust of an incredibly passionate team of professionals, friends, and family members.

Writing about icons such as Walt Disney and Van France and the institutions they created is a task not casually undertaken. Executives who spent decades in the Walt Disney Company—for many, it was their entire career—shared openly with me their experiences with Walt and Van. Some were my former managers at Disney, some occupied positions many levels above, others were colleagues and teammates, and all were contributors to *Disney U*. I deeply value the gift of trust they bestowed on me to accurately convey the information they provided.

Without collaboration and teamwork, this project would have never come to completion. Yet without the support of one person in particular, this project would never have even gotten off the ground. I must offer my sincerest thank you to Jim Cora, the retired chairman of Disneyland International. *Disney U* wouldn't have been possible without his support. Throughout his long and distinguished career, Jim created countless opportunities for many Disney cast members, including me. Jim, as a matter-of-fact leader, expected and provided absolute dedication. Jim learned directly from Van—and from Walt himself—that Walt's philosophy of "maintain quality, keep the park clean, and keep it friendly" also meant being absolutely dedicated to the product, the Disney show. I always knew Jim to be a tough but fair boss. During my many interactions with him during the course of writing *Disney U*, I learned about a whole different side of Jim; he is a romantic at heart. During a meeting at his home, Jim pointed out a unique feature of which he is most proud. It isn't the expanse of beautifully landscaped grounds, nor is it the custom-built garage in which he restores classic cars. He is most proud of the grapevines climbing the fence in his backyard. Jim, of Lebanese descent, proudly shared with me the story of how his grandmother brought from the old country the rootstock that now flourishes in his yard.

Many others offered their valuable time by giving advice or in many cases sharing compelling personal stories about their Disney experiences. Each enthusiastically supported the project and encouraged me to write about Van and the Disney University. The overwhelming response I received can be summed up in a statement made by all: "It's about time someone wrote about Van. His story needs to be shared!" These gracious former Disney executives are Dick Cook, Carol Davis-Fernald, Thor Degelmann, Bob De Nayer, Ron Dominguez, Tom Eastman, Jeff Hoffman, Steve Lewelling, Jack Lindquist, Kris McNamara, Darrell Metzger, Ron Miller, Ron Pogue, Bill Ross, Marty Sklar, Craig Smith, Dave Smith, Dianna Stark, and Mike Vance. Carol, Bob, and Dave: thank you for your unending patience when I would write or call with "just one more question."

Transforming ideas and mountains of notes into a book is a gargantuan task. Sam Fleishman, my literary agent, provided countless hours of coaching and was a rock-solid source of information and inspiration. Sam's rich professional background, including his years as a professor of film and media studies as well as a film and TV producer, provided the perfect balance of discipline and creativity.

Mary Glenn, associate publisher at McGraw-Hill Professional, and her wonderfully talented team ensured that the message remained on target. Michael Bergdahl, a gifted author, business leader, and valued friend, encouraged me to embrace the risk of writing about an iconic figure.

The following individuals provided tremendous support in helping me with everything from suggesting additional resources to verifying the accuracy of data, timelines, and statistics: Art Agnos, Dave Beeman, Gail Brown, Marilyn Buckhoff, Mike Buckhoff, Lynette Campbell, Kevin Corcoran, Mary Beth Culler, Diane Deacon, David Gordon, Kathy Gunter, Bruce Landry, Lee Lanselle, Nancy Montgomery, Sarah Rezmovitz, Steven Vagnini, and Dan Wolf.

Patti Newman helped me remain patient and find my voice. Al Gianini posed just the right questions. Lorrie Beeman helped with many taxing issues. To those who prefer not to be named, I am deeply grateful for your help.

One of the highlights of working on this book was the time I spent with Ron Miller and Diane Disney Miller. Diane embodies the passion of her father, Walt, and has created a most fitting tribute to his legacy: The Walt Disney Family Museum. The museum, a gem of Disney heritage situated at the Presidio in San Francisco, California, is a whimsical and deeply thought-provoking acknowledgment of Walt's accomplishments and values.

As always, family members gave me the gifts of patience, encouragement, and love. At times, I felt like Rip Van Winkle, emerging from my time warp of a writer's cave unshaven and with bloodshot eyes, looking for nourishment, both caloric and spiritual. My family unfailingly provided both. My parents, Gordon and Polly Lipp, and my kids, Allison, Amanda, and Keith, all patiently offered support and advice. The suggestions they gave during our many discussions—over dinner, via e-mail, during family camping trips—have made *Disney U* much more reader-friendly.

The person who deserves the most appreciation for offering support, patience, creativity, and love is my wife, Pam. From the earliest days of brainstorming ideas through the interminable hours of editing, Pam has been a constant source of strength. Pam is my partner in business and in life, my best friend and confidante. It helps that she also spent years working at Disney.

Pam's Disney career began at Disneyland in merchandise and as a candy maker at the Candy Palace on Main Street and then as a tour guide. Pam transferred from Disneyland to the Disney Studio to pursue a career planning employee recreational events at the Mickey Mouse Activity Center (yes, a real place!), a department in the Disney University. After a two-year assignment in Japan as part of the start-up team for Tokyo Disneyland, I accepted a position in training at the Disney University at the Studio. Perhaps as a result of karma, fate, or sheer luck, Pam and I began our Disney Studio assignments just three days apart in November 1983. Nearly three decades later, Pam and I share a fulfilling life running our consulting business and enjoying our three adult children.

A Note from the Author

Van France, *"a strange combination of Jiminy Cricket, Mary Poppins, and Donald Duck"*

It was an evening I'll always remember. We peppered Van with an unending stream of questions:

"What was it like working with Walt?"

"How different would Disneyland be today if Walt were still with us?"

"What would Walt do?"

"What would Walt say?"

"What kind of a leader was Walt?"

We asked Van these and many more questions about the old days, when he worked directly with Walt Disney. It was a rare opportunity for us to interact with one of the true living legends of the company, and we were bound and determined to make the most of it. Van was patient—even gracious at first—as he responded to the kinds of questions he had undoubtedly answered thousands of times before. I don't remember which question actually set him off—perhaps it was the one asking him to lay out his vision for the company's future—but in an instant, he went from a polite elderly statesman to a whirling ball of profane energy. In his inimitable style, he began a rapid-fire pattern of alternately sharing his favorite quotes from Walt and then challenging us. "How the hell would I know? You're supposed to be the future leaders of this place! What do *you* think?" We had just witnessed the infamous passion and temper of Van France, the founder of the Disney University.

We were gathered in the main theater of the Disney University at Disneyland, the very institution Van helped create. I was one of 20 leadership interns in that audience, each representing one of the various operating divisions of the company. We had been chosen to participate in a rigorous six-month leadership training camp known as the Disney Management Intern Program. Most of us were in our middle to late twenties and thrilled to be participating in a program designed to groom the future leaders of the company. In his role as featured guest speaker, Van kicked off the program, and he did an admirable job of setting the tone. He gave us a personal account of what it meant to work directly for Walt Disney and what he learned from such an amazingly creative, always demanding, laser-focused, and charismatic leader. For most of us in the room, that evening marked the beginning of a most intense and rewarding leadership journey. As the current and future leaders of the company, how would we keep alive the dreams, the passions, and the focus of Walt Disney?

Fortunately for me, this wasn't the only time I met Van. Among the 20 interns, I was one of the two assigned to the human resources division. Since the Disney University is part of the HR division, I had plenty of additional chances to interact with Van. My career goal was to be in management at the Disney University, and so I spent a lot of my time as an intern learning as much as possible from the trainers and managers of the university, including Van.

What is the connection to Jiminy Cricket, Mary Poppins, and Donald Duck?[1] This spot-on description of Van is shared by many who worked with him, in particular Dick Nunis, the former chairman of Walt Disney Parks and Resorts and board member of The

Walt Disney Company. Dick would know; he was the first person Van hired at Disneyland. Van brought Dick on board to help him design the very first Disney employee orientation and training program. Walt needed employees who would "create happiness," and it was up to Van and his new employee, Dick, to lead the charge.

Jiminy Cricket is well known for tirelessly offering positive encouragement to Pinocchio, directing him onto a more honest path—even after Pinocchio repeatedly ignores his advice. Mary Poppins, as the nanny of two spirited children, is famous for coaxing them to do the right thing by singing, "A spoonful of sugar helps the medicine go down." Similarly to these two characters, Van was a moral compass for the company. But his style couldn't have been more different from those of the patient Jiminy Cricket and the genteel Mary Poppins. Van's style was similar to that of Donald Duck, the beloved character well known for his bursts of temper. Like the irascible Donald, Van was quick to give an earful of criticism to anyone who was not perpetuating Walt's dream.[2]

Van, at about five feet eight inches tall and perhaps 135 pounds—dripping wet—was larger than life. He believed passionately in Walt's dream and demanded the same passion from those around him. In fact, Van was actually a lot like Walt himself. Walt's dream of creating a place offering a most unique family entertainment experience—Disneyland—was mirrored by Van's dream of creating a place offering a most unique employee education experience—the Disney University.

During his 30-plus years with the company, Van experienced the many ups and downs that come with corporate life. He saw firsthand some of the spectacular successes—and failures—of The Walt Disney Company. He learned from those experiences and, always the trainer, was quick to share his opinions.

Armed with a clear vision and leadership support and surrounded by an immensely talented team, Van France created an institution that continues to define excellence and unparalleled success. The Disney University plays a major role in turning out employees who are second to none when it comes to friendliness, knowledge, attentiveness, passion, and guest service. Disney theme parks and resorts around the world are the main attraction; the Disney University trains the supporting cast that helps create the world-famous Disney Magic.

Van France, professor emeritus Disney Universities, was a creative dynamo. The leadership lessons he shared with so many generations of Disney employees are more important now than ever before. Van, a strange combination of three of Disney's most famous characters—Jiminy Cricket, Mary Poppins, and Donald Duck—exuded qualities and values every leader should strive to attain: crystal-clear direction plus an unwavering commitment and passion.

Van France died in 1999. His leadership lessons are alive and well.

—Doug Lipp
January 13, 2013

"Help Me Create 'The Happiest Place on Earth'"

The message to Van was clear:

> *We need you to mold a group of diverse Californians, with no business experience, into producers of the "Disneyland Dream."*[1]

With these words, Van France, professor emeritus and founder of the University of Disneyland—now called Disney University— was charged with the task of helping Walt Disney create "The Happiest Place on Earth."

This was in early 1955, and Walt Disney's dream of creating a world of fantasy—a *theme park*—where young and old alike could have fun in a family-friendly atmosphere, was finally coming true. The grand opening of Disneyland, scheduled for July 17, 1955, was just months away, and Walt needed Van's help.

Walt had assembled some of the brightest minds of the time to design and build his park, and they were working at breakneck speed to complete it. The transformation had already begun; what once were acres of orange groves in Anaheim, California, were now fanciful attractions and buildings soon to be known as Disneyland. In essence, the stage was nearing completion, and it would be Van's job to supply the cast to run the show. Walt was building a one-of-a-kind place, now he needed passionate people to work there.[2]

Walt Disney had plenty of architects for the buildings. What he desperately needed now was someone like Van—someone to be the *human architect*, someone who could be as creative designing the employee orientation and training process as the *real* architects had been with their landscape and building designs. It was up to Van and his team to develop employees who could "create happiness." At 42 years of age, Van France already had plenty of experience as a trainer in manufacturing companies and in the military. He had just been given the opportunity of a lifetime.

Van first met Walt, six months earlier, at the Disney Studio complex in Burbank, California. The meeting was held in the Animation Building, home to all the artists and executives who brought Walt's dreams to life. It was also where Walt Disney's office was located. According to Van, "I parked in the visitors' lot and set off on foot down Snow White Lane, past Dopey Drive, until I came to Mickey Mouse Avenue and the Studio's three-story Animation Building."[3] Van noticed immediately that this was a different sort of organization. This work environment was worlds apart from where he had spent the bulk of his career; as a training specialist with the U.S. Army, in an auto assembly plant, and when he had been in charge of training at an aircraft factory. He had even worked as a consultant at a brassiere factory.[4]

At that time, the Disney Studio had a wonderfully relaxed feel. A large canopy of trees protected the beautifully maintained buildings, many in the *art moderne* style so popular when the Studio was built in the late 1930s.[5] Van learned later that this architectural style, which incorporated long horizontal windows into the design, allowed an abundance of natural light into the Animation Building—an asset to the artists and animators. The well-manicured lawns, dotted with park benches, only added to the feeling that this was a college campus, not the headquarters of a corporation poised to forever change the business world.

This was the beginning of a second career for Van Arsdale France—one that would become legendary. The pressure Van felt that day was no different from what managers, business owners, and leaders feel today—produce or get out of the way. Van knew that Walt had already poured many years and millions of his own dollars into a project that an army of experts predicted would be a financial failure. He wanted to help Walt prove the skeptics wrong. He accepted the challenge to work on Walt's dream.

By helping Walt Disney create The Happiest Place on Earth, Van France and his dedicated team started a business revolution in 1955 that eventually became the Disney University—an institution that forever changed the profession of employee training and development. Along the way, Van and his team learned and shared many lessons about creativity, flexibility, and change, about leadership and sustainability. From the hectic months and days preceding the grand opening of Disneyland through the ensuing decades of growth, there was an abundance of heady success, plus some gut-wrenching challenges. Those turned out to be valuable lessons for Disney leadership and Van. Ever the keen observer of human behavior, Van was quick to challenge the Disney University team and company leaders to transform those events into learning opportunities and lessons—to maximize the successes and minimize the failures. Those lessons are the essence of this book.

Van France would be the first person to say he didn't create these lessons; he wouldn't hesitate to divert attention from himself. After all, how many times had he repeated Walt's famous quote to legions of new employees?

"Disneyland is the star; everything else is in the supporting role."[6]

Van would probably attribute the value that resides in each and every lesson to the brilliance of Walt Disney. Van would also be quick to give credit to the talented team of pioneers in The Walt Disney Company and in the Disney University.

Van and his team didn't always agree, but they learned from each other. The complexity within Walt's request of Van, "Help me create 'The Happiest Place on Earth'" is mind-boggling. Van is the one who took those orders and made them manageable. Comments made by Walt Disney Company executives and Disney University pioneers, who worked with or for Van, echo versions of the same sentiment:

> "To this day, I am amazed by how Van made the inherently complex so simple. This does not mean simplistic or 'dumbed down.'"

> "Van took theoretical messages and made them digestible, understandable, actionable and sustainable."[7]

> "Van had the uncanny ability to articulate the complex."

> "Van made learning fun."

Finally, in addition to Walt, there is one other person whom Van would credit as *the* driving force behind the Disney University—Dick Nunis. Dick, the former chairman of Walt Disney Parks and Resorts and board member of The Walt Disney Company, was originally hired by Van to be his assistant. In later years, their roles reversed and Van reported to Dick. Their dynamic relationship spanned many decades, and together they brought Walt's dream to life through the Disney University.

More than a half century after they were first introduced, the Disney University lessons continue to be alive and well at Disney properties worldwide. These lessons are timeless.

Pulling Back the Curtain: The Orientation

What happens "backstage" will end up "on-stage." If we aren't friendly with each other . . . smiling and saying "good morning" and things like that, then we'll have a similar attitude toward our guests.[1]

—Van Arsdale France, founder and
professor emeritus, Disney Universities

Disney University, 5 p.m.

Sophie sat in the training room and couldn't keep the smile from her face. In fact, her cheeks were sore from all the smiling and laughing she had done in the last eight hours. The orientation program had just ended. She was now a graduate of the Disney University and ready to go out and create The Happiest Place on Earth.

Sure, it had been a long day, but it didn't feel like it. The more she thought about it—her first day as a Disney cast member—the more it started making sense. She thought about everything she had experienced; the presentations by the staff, the videos, the tour of the park, and finally her interaction with the other trainees. A full day of information had flown by. "Although there was a lot of serious stuff, what was it that made this experience so enjoyable?" she wondered. What caused her to feel so motivated and eager to run out the door to do her job?

"What time is the three o'clock parade?" "Where is my car parked?" Who on earth would ask such silly questions? she thought. Sophie understood that guests would ask, "Where's Mickey Mouse?" or "Where is the restroom?" But a question about the *three o'clock parade*? You have to be kidding! Well, according to Hector and Monica, the two orientation trainers, a lot of people who visit Disneyland were likely to ask those very questions and many more. It was now up to her and everyone else in that room—all the other new hires sitting around her—to answer those questions with smiles on their faces and in their friendly voices.

"It is all about putting on the best 'show' for our guests," said Hector. "You are now part of that show, which is the reason we refer to each other as 'cast members' and not 'employees.' We are all part of the cast in the show called Disneyland."

Monica and Hector referred to examples of "show" and "cast" throughout the day. They would say, "Here is an example of what we call good show" while displaying a picture of a cast member interacting with a guest. They would then ask everyone, "So what makes this an example of good show?" At first, Sophie and her fellow trainees couldn't identify every example in the picture, but by the end of the orientation program, they all saw the pattern: the cast member was always smiling, his or her clothing was spotless, and if the cast member was giving the guest directions (to the restroom, perhaps), his or her hand was always open and inviting, not pointing the way with an index finger. Sophie never saw a picture or video that showed cast members frowning, wearing dirty or wrinkled clothing, or rudely pointing the way with a finger unless Monica and Hector were giving examples—which they often did— of the opposite of good show, the Disney taboo known as bad show.

But what was so different about Sophie's experience today?

Sophie began to recall specific examples of how Hector, Monica, and the whole training staff had delivered good show to the trainees. The uplifting music playing in the lobby when she arrived that morning was a nice touch. She appreciated the way they greeted her when she walked into the building. In fact, she arrived 30 minutes before the start of the orientation, and the staff was ready to go; no last-minute rushing around or the flurry of activity so common before the start of training programs. Their smiles, plus everyone saying, "Good morning; welcome to the Disney University," was a nice way to start the day. Of course, who could resist smiling when the song "Hakuna Matata" from *The Lion King* is blaring in the background? Sophie also admitted to herself that she'd had doubts that morning about the sincerity of those smiles. Surely the training staff can't keep up this act all day, she'd thought. And even if they can, they're *paid* to be friendly; that's their job. That had been eight hours earlier, and since then she had seen, heard, and experienced a lot. It was all starting to make sense.

Sophie appreciated Monica's and Hector's honesty when they said that producing The Happiest Place on Earth day after day is hard work for the cast members. Throughout the day they said in one way or another, "This might sound like an obvious statement, but working here is *work*; it's a lot harder providing the show than enjoying the show as a guest." Sophie liked their balanced approach; they were a smiling bunch, but they weren't sugarcoating anything.

The Two Worlds of Disney

For Sophie, the classroom sessions were engaging, but actually *touring* the park—returning to the oasis of her childhood bliss—was the moment on the training schedule she had been anticipating since hour 1. Sophie had been to Disneyland many times as a guest, and so she was familiar with many of the attractions, the gift shops, and the general layout. But during the tour, the information and special

jargon introduced earlier by the trainers in the training room became a reality. She now had a completely different perspective.

Just before leaving the room for the tour, Monica asked all the
trainees to pay particular attention to the two worlds of Disney: on-
stage and backstage: "The backstage area is a world our guests never
see. On-stage is the area many of you experienced as guests over
the years. For example, this orientation room is backstage, as are all
the hallways we will walk through on our way to the on-stage area."

After leaving the training room, Monica and Hector led all of
them through the backstage area to an innocuous gate. Just before
going through the gate, Hector said, "We are still in the backstage
area. Take a good look around and make a mental note of what you
see. We'll conclude the tour here, but first, follow me." Hector then
led them through the gate. Suddenly, they were in Tomorrowland,
surrounded by guests and looking at Space Mountain looming
above.

"We are now on-stage," said Monica. "This is where our guests
experience a Disney park or resort, where the attractions, restaurants, shops, and restrooms are located." She explained that any
area where the guest comes into contact with a cast member or
the Disney property is part of the show and is called on-stage. She
summed up this comment by saying, "On-stage is, quite frankly, the
only thing customers know and care about."

Monica continued: "Most guests don't have any idea about our
attention to detail, the things we consider when creating the show.
For example, the sidewalks in Disneyland don't have 90-degree
corners. Think about it. Have any of us ever arrived at a sidewalk
intersection and made a precise 90-degree turn? None of us do!
That's why our sidewalks are curved; they are designed with people
in mind—with the way people move. People tend to meander, not
march, and our sidewalks complement that tendency."

"You are now seeing Disneyland from a totally different perspective," Hector added. "In fact, please focus on some additional details
as we continue our tour of the on-stage area." As they approached

Main Street, Hector pointed out the height of the windows in the shops and arcades lining both sides of the street. "Every storefront on Main Street is designed with a child in mind. The windows are low enough to the sidewalk to allow even a small child to easily look into the shop without having to stand on his or her toes. Walt Disney actually viewed the park from a child's perspective during the construction phase. Often he squatted down to assess an attraction or building from the height of a child and then posed this question to his planners: 'Can you see little kids looking up at this?'"[2]

Moments later, Hector led them through yet another well-disguised gate, this one marked with a CAST MEMBERS ONLY sign. Once again, they were backstage. There Sophie learned the vital role this whole other world plays in putting on the Disney Show. She would never forget the tour of this area of the park. All the cast members' break rooms, locker rooms, and cafeterias intrigued her.

Hector then gave an analogy that clarified the difference between backstage and on-stage: "Backstage, while organized and well maintained, isn't *spotless* like our on-stage areas. Think of when you entertain guests in your home or apartment. Don't most of you straighten up your place a bit before your guests arrive? You might put the vacuum cleaner in a closet, load dishes in the dishwasher, and shove your clothes in the back room, right? In other words, you get the clutter out of your guests' sight. So you can consider your closet, the back room, and the dishwasher as the backstage areas of your home. While our backstage area is much larger and more complicated than those areas of your home, it has much the same function: it separates the world we want our guests to see from the world we want to keep private."

Sophie not only learned that backstage is the sole domain of the cast members of a Disney park or resort but also learned about its importance in maintaining good show. Backstage is where maintenance and operations personnel can access the attractions if something needs to be fixed. This is where trucks delivering food and merchandise arrive and depart undetected. Cast members come here to recharge their batteries, which usually are completely drained after answering the three o'clock parade question all day long. Sophie was shocked when she saw a cast member wolfing down a hamburger and drinking a soda. Just moments before, she had been a beautiful princess on-stage. It really hit home when she saw the Goofy character walking by, taking off his head. Of course, she thought. Real people are inside those costumes. But there was no denying the shock value of seeing it with her own eyes. Hector and Monica knew how this affected trainees and used every opportunity to make their point. Monica took full advantage of this by saying, "There goes Goofy to take a well-deserved break. Guests will never see him like that; our backstage world never seeps on-stage." She reinforced this message by asking the group, "And why wouldn't this ever happen?"

Almost in unison, the trainees responded, "It would be bad show on-stage."

"Exactly," Hector said as he continued with the same theme. "Now, I'd like all of you to think about some recent experiences you've had as a customer. When, where, and how often did you experience bad show when you interacted with service providers? When did you see or hear backstage behavior in a public on-stage environment?"

Sophie considered the question. She remembered hearing the clerk at the supermarket complain about the boss to a coworker. She also recalled a telephone call to a computer technician that didn't go well; the technician had no patience and constantly interrupted her. Even her doctor's receptionist never looked up to acknowledge her entrance. Sophie realized how often she had experienced bad show behavior just in the last week. It was the equivalent of Goofy taking off his head, multiple times, on-stage.

Good show, bad show thoughts swirled through Sophie's head. The stories about viewing things from the perspective of the guest—curved sidewalks and child-friendly windows—introduced powerful concepts about guest service. Those things, however, are just part of the story. Why are the cast members so friendly? And why couldn't the receptionist at her doctor's office smile and greet her?

Monica's subsequent comments gave Sophie valuable insight. "As we've discussed all day, Disney is known for guest service, and we're proud of this. We know the value of incorporating the guests' perception when creating our attractions and buildings. In addition, we firmly believe that the best way to offer outstanding service to our guests is to first provide it to our employees. Our cast members are our number one customer. The show our guests experience on-stage is a direct reflection of what happens back here. Treating each other with respect and greeting each other backstage with a smile are just as important as our world-famous characters and attractions."

There was a moment of silence. Then Monica wrapped up this key learning point by adding, "We take care of the cast, the cast takes care of our guests, and our business thrives."

Sophie couldn't keep track of all the helpful information she was acquiring on the tour. Seeing the challenge of putting on such a complex show brought to life the ideas the training staff had presented that morning. One minute, Hector and Monica fired questions at them. The next, they encouraged everyone to consider guest service from new perspectives. Not a moment passed in which Sophie lost engagement. And it was fun.

A Lesson from Mr. Lincoln

While still pondering the whole good show versus bad show message, Sophie thought about another part of the tour she really appreciated. It was during their visit to the Disneyland Opera House on Disneyland's Main Street. Hector and Monica escorted them to that theater, where they watched the Audio-Animatronic show *Great Moments with Mr. Lincoln*. Sophie thought that the show was interesting, as were the displays and drawings in the lobby of the theater—referred to by the Disney trainers as the preshow area (there was that "show" word again). It fascinated her.

Monica then instructed all the trainees to pay particular attention to the displays. "This is called *The Walt Disney Story*. It introduces the history of Disneyland. We'll discuss your observations once we return to the orientation room."

Sophie enjoyed the pictures depicting how Disneyland appeared when it first opened. The scale models of the buildings and the artists' renderings of Walt Disney's original ideas for the park layout were stunning. It was like a museum tour. As an added benefit, the 15-minute wait time for the *Great Moments with Mr. Lincoln* show flew by because she was so intrigued by the displays in the preshow area.

When they returned to the orientation room, Hector and Monica impressed Sophie with the way they engaged everyone in a discussion about the preshow displays and the *Great Moments with Mr. Lincoln* show. "We take all new cast members through this same tour and exercise," Monica said. "We believe it is important for you to know about our history, where we came from, in order to appreciate where we are today. Hector and I are proud to be part of the Disney tradition of excellence and hope you leave today with a similar feeling of pride. It is up to all of us to help the company move forward."[3]

Sophie wasn't quite sure where they were going with this idea when, as if on cue, Monica shared more history about the *Great Moments with Mr. Lincoln* show. "Speaking of the past and how it influences the present and the future, we want to tell you a little bit more about the Mr. Lincoln attraction." She explained how *Great Moments with Mr. Lincoln* was created by Disney for the 1964 New York World's Fair. Sponsored by the state of Illinois, it was the featured attraction at that pavilion. "Mr. Lincoln was one of the first full-sized human Audio-Animatronics figures developed by Disney," Monica continued. "In fact, the technology was so new that it was still being perfected right up until the show was unveiled."

Hector then asked the group, "So why are we telling you about something that happened so many years ago?"

"To reinforce Disney's groundbreaking technology?" offered one.

"So we appreciate the teamwork required for creating the show?" others added.

Sophie and some of the other trainees suggested a few more reasons, but no one could have predicted the answer the trainers were seeking. Hector thanked them for their ideas and said, "There was a lot riding on the success of the *Great Moments with Mr. Lincoln* attraction. The state of Illinois paid a lot of money for its development, and Walt Disney's pride and the credibility of his company were on the line."

Hector added, "Walt and his team of imagineers held a preview of the show two days before the grand opening.[4] The Lincoln Theater was full; 500 dignitaries from Illinois plus members of the press from around the world were waiting for the big moment. The governor of Illinois was already on stage introducing the show. But there was a problem." At this point in the story, Hector paused for dramatic effect, then added, "There was a technical malfunction; the show didn't work as planned. And in spite of tremendous pressure to let the show go on, Walt Disney canceled it. Walt actually came on stage, told the audience about the problem, and then let them know that the show wouldn't be running that evening." Hector went on to explain that the problem was eventually fixed—it took about a week—and the show did go on. But an important point had been made. Walt was willing to suffer momentary embarrassment and sustain short-term pain for long-term gain. Certainly, Walt's on-stage announcement could be viewed as bad show. What concerned Walt most was accurately depicting President Lincoln in Audio-Animatronic form.

For Sophie, this story was a summation of all the messages that day: Walt was not willing to sacrifice show quality. The focus on good show versus bad show and on-stage versus backstage became clear. Disneyland is a giant stage, and we—the cast members—are part of that show. Walt was a stickler for details. Now, many decades later, we were receiving the same message: don't put on a show until every element is checked and rechecked.

Connecting at All Levels

As the day drew to a close, Monica asked, "Who would like to share with us your first impression from this morning? What did you *experience*? What did you *feel* when you came into this room?"

"You were all smiling," said several trainees at the same time.

"I liked the music and the fun atmosphere!" one yelled.

"Yeah, the posters of Mickey, Donald and Buzz Lightyear really helped," said another.

Another piped in, "The bathrooms are spotless."

Sophie offered, "I felt welcomed."

"Thank you!" shouted Monica. "Our goal today was to appeal to you at an intellectual *and* emotional level. For example, we prepared the training room last night, well before your arrival. You are our guests, and we made sure our stage was set. Did you notice how all of the desks and chairs were perfectly aligned even when you returned from breaks? For those of you who arrived early, you didn't see Hector, the staff, or me rushing around, did you? When you walked in, 100 percent of our focus was on *you*." Sophie thought about this comment, then shared an observation with the trainers and staff, who were now all standing at the front of the room: "You did this the whole day, not just this morning. You modeled respectful behavior to us just as we will do with guests once we start working. Your attention to all of these details helped me relax. I had fun, plus I learned a lot. Thanks."

Hector began his wrap-up: "We know this has been a long day, and we gave you a lot of information. We hope the mixture of facts and fun, plus the film clips and our mini field trip into the park, made it all the more memorable. And believe it or not, your training has just begun. In a few minutes, I'll introduce to you a new team of trainers. These folks are known as our university leaders. They represent the areas where each of you will work, and their job is to guide you through several more days of job-specific training."

Monica then stepped forward to close the program with these last thoughts: "Our goal with any orientation is to use the whole experience as an introduction to the Disney Show. We modeled the same environment we provide our guests at each of our theme parks and resorts; the stage is always set, and cast members are always friendly. This is why guests keep coming back. Our survey data reveal what guests value in a Disney experience, *why* they return so frequently. In order of priority, guests tell us it's our *friendliness, cleanliness,* and *safety.*"[5]

Sophie couldn't have been more surprised. Before attending this orientation program, she would have bet guests' lists of favorite things would focus on the Disney characters, parades, and attractions.

"Think about it," Hector added. "Had we been inattentive or rude to you today, would you be excited about going to work? If this training room was a mess and the bathrooms dirty, would you have believed our message about the importance of cleanliness? Of course not! You value the same things as our guests. Our cast members are friendly and engaged; our parks and resorts are clean, organized, and orderly; and we all enjoy a safe environment." He paused for a few seconds, then shouted, "Welcome to Disney!"

Sophie was officially a graduate of the Disney University orientation program. Yet in spite of her enthusiasm, she knew this didn't mean she could run out the door and immediately interact with guests. She still needed to attend several more days of on-the-job training designed and taught by a team in the division where she would be working. The university leader introduced moments before by Hector represented her division and would be leading her next phase of training. Sophie looked forward to the day when she could return to the Disney University to learn more. When she took courses to improve her guest service skills or prepare for an eventual job as a supervisor, Sophie was confident they would be as informative and enjoyable as today's orientation program.

She was now part of the team charged with creating The Happiest Place on Earth, and she was more than excited about starting work. Many questions had been answered during her orientation, but she had many more. How long would it take for her enthusiasm to wear off? What would she learn from her coworkers once she actually started working? Would they share with her something that would unravel all the positive messages of this day?

Sophie's lingering questions were no different from those asked by the tens of thousands of cast members who had come before her. And the answers to her questions wouldn't appear while she was sitting in the orientation room at the Disney University. Ultimately, she would learn that there is much more to the Disney Magic than new-hire orientation. This was just the beginning. The answers to her questions would come—just as they had for so many others— once she started her job.

"How does Disney do it?"

"How do they keep their employees so motivated and engaged?"

"What's the Disney *secret*?"

Setting the Stage for Success

The Four Circumstances of the Disney University

It took more than a good idea to bring the university into existence. This new baby in the corporate family might have died in the delivery room had it not been for certain circumstances.[1]

—**Van France**

MEMORANDUM

September 21, 1962

Disneyland will never be completed. We've certainly lived up to that promise. But what about the people who operate it? Are we growing with the show or just getting older? The trouble with people is that we get hardening of the mental arteries, cirrhosis of the enthusiasm, and arthritis of the imagination, along with chronic and sometimes acute allergies to supervision, subordinates, the whole darned system. Is it possible that what we have gained through experience, we have lost through habit, and that what we have gained through organization, we have lost in enthusiasm?

—Van France, Introduction to his "Proposed Program for the University of Disneyland, 1962–1963"[2]

Setting the Stage for
The Disney University

In 1955, just before Disneyland's grand opening, Van France and his only employee at the time, a new college graduate named Dick Nunis, originated the very first Disneyland employee orientation program. It produced legions of employees who by the end of orientation had no doubt about their primary role with the guests who were soon to arrive: "We create happiness."

Right from its debut on July 17, 1955, Disneyland enjoyed unparalleled success. It raised the bar, setting new standards of excellence for creativity, family entertainment, and customer service.

In the years since it opened, Disneyland evolved in a variety of ways, from the number and complexity of attractions to the expanding employee population. Van also evolved. He left Disneyland for two years to work for other companies. When he returned in 1962, he was looking at Disneyland from a new perspective. Van says, "My learning in the outside world helped me. I could now look at Disneyland with fresh insights."[3] He discovered a Disneyland that was facing some growing pains.

Deteriorating employee morale was especially troubling to Van. There were even complaints about the orientation program; some argued that the material was dated and that those presenting it were out of touch with the realities of the park operations.[4]

During Van's two-year hiatus, Dick Nunis, Van's only employee during the months before and after the opening of Disneyland, became the director of operations at Disneyland. Dick, now Van's boss, needed his help.

Seven years into this run of success and millions of guests later, Van France began thinking about expanding the Disneyland orientation program to something new and different. The time was right for this new baby in the Disney corporate family to emerge.

The Disney University was about to be born.

Beyond a University in Name Only: The Four Circumstances

The Disney University is a name that carries clout and evokes images of excellence. Mention this highly regarded institution to any business leader, and the question that often follows is: How do they develop the world's most engaged, loyal, and customer-centric employees, year after year?

The simple explanation for the Disney University's success can be attributed to the levels of support and clarity of purpose found in the Four Circumstances, the organizational values Van France identified as vital to the success of the Disney University.[5]

Although the word *university* invariably appears in the title of corporate and organizational training departments around the world, very few of those "universities" have matched the Disney University's level of success. Many don't enjoy the levels of support and clarity of purpose found in the Four Circumstances. Without clarifying the kinds of values found in the Four Circumstances, training and development initiatives are bound to fail; even the best-funded organizational universities are doomed to become universities in name only.

Van's Four Circumstances Are Values

The ensuing review of each circumstance reveals key words that represent values of The Walt Disney Company and create the perfect environment for the Disney University. But before discussing the values that constitute Van's Four Circumstances, it is important to first clarify something about them:

- These values are not unique.

- These values aren't new or unknown to most leaders.

- These values must pervade the organization. They are the essential DNA of the whole company, not just Van's values or those of the Disney University.

These core values, which were originally set into motion by Walt Disney, form a sturdy foundation from which evolved the programs Van and his team developed. The Disney University is an extension of the company.[6]

Put simply, the Disney University isn't a car wash through which employees can be sent in preparation for work.[7] It is much, much more. A sentiment shared by many executives who worked with Van is, "Training cannot be limited to 'Here's what you need to do, now go do it.' That's not good enough. Training needs to instill a spirit, a feeling, an emotional connection. Training means creating an environment of thinking and feeling."

Van's Circumstance 1: Innovation

First, I had an aversion to the concept of a "training department." The function has little status in any organization. Years before, when I had actually managed a "training department," I grew tired of hearing, "Those who can, do; those who can't, teach." Further, any high school graduate feels he or she has already been trained and resents being enrolled again. On the other hand, the idea of a University was exciting. Historically, a university was ahead of the times, leading people into exciting adventures.[8]

This circumstance reveals the traits associated with those who break new ground: the pioneers who are not afraid to take risks. Van's focus on being innovative created an ever-evolving learning culture. He challenged the status quo.

Many who worked with Van describe his style in the following ways:

"Van kept people focused. He kept us from making training programs too esoteric and academic by keeping us focused on practical application, using simple concepts such as 'we create happiness' and 'we know the answers.'"

"He brought up pointed and controversial ideas that kept us thinking."

"Van made sure we didn't get too infatuated with our own importance or success."[9]

"Van had a good way of deflating your balloon."[10]

Van's zeal for creating The Happiest Place on Earth through innovation and by challenging entrenched behavioral patterns and beliefs is evident in a passage he created for an early 1980s Disneyland management training program:

Budgets, schedules, reports, more reports, union negotiations, training programs, meetings . . . more meetings, handbooks, "cover-your-ass" memos and the endless things which take up your time are of no value unless they end up producing A HAPPY GUEST.[11]

Van didn't hesitate to stir the pot.

Van's Circumstance 2: Organizational Support

Second, Dick's [*Dick Nunis, the then director of operations at Disneyland*] degree from USC was in education and he could see the advantages of branching out from a simple orientation program. Further, after Dick buys an idea, he backs it and sells it.[12]

This circumstance adds a component that is lacking in too many organizations; unabashed organizational support. From Walt and

Roy Disney and then to Dick Nunis, Disney management trusted Van's ideas and he trusted them.

Dick knew that unless someone from the highest ranks of management backs it, it won't happen; leadership must be intimately involved and has to set the tone. Dick's constant presence as a champion of training started at Disneyland and continued with the development of Walt Disney World in Florida and the international expansion of Disney Parks and Resorts.

When Van proposed creating the Disney University, Dick became one of his biggest cheerleaders and encouraged him to run with his ideas. Van's words are echoed in the following statement, a sentiment voiced by Disney University pioneers:

> *Without the support of Walt Disney and Dick Nunis, there wouldn't be a Disney University.*[13]

Van's Circumstance 3: Education

Third, back in 1932, Walt had established his own, unique school for training his animators, and he could understand why we had to develop our own breed of spectacular show people.[14]

Without a doubt, this circumstance reveals the roots of the Disney University: Walt's long-standing value of providing employees with a tailored, relevant training and educational experience. Walt Disney helped create an art school for his animators because in his own words, "Art schools that existed then didn't quite have enough for what we needed, so we set up our own art school . . . we went a little bit beyond what they were getting in art school."[15]

Walt often brought into the studio prominent educators and artists such as Frank Lloyd Wright to give classes and lectures to the animators. Their innovative ideas and outside-the-box thinking became an invaluable source of inspiration.[16]

Van had to create a different version of Walt's art school: a unique school that would create a different type of artist. These "Disneylanders" would major in the fine art of creating happiness and receive a special curriculum in human relations and Disney philosophy.[17] Van and his fellow pioneers knew they had to create something that would go beyond traditional training programs. There was no question that the main product at Disneyland was going to be happiness. There was no ambiguity in the look, feel, and purpose of the goal.

When it is offered consistently and with creativity, education is an indispensable commodity, one that is held in high esteem in the history and culture of The Walt Disney Company.

Van's Circumstance 4: Entertain

Finally, fourth, I had friendly allies in the Art Department of the Marketing division. As result, our handbooks and training aids were always creative and interesting, rather than the opposite, which would mean "dull and academic."[18]

Van's description of this circumstance illustrates his firm belief in a value he shared with Walt: entertain *and* educate. As Walt would say, "When the subject permits, we let fly with all the satire and gags at our command. Laughter is no enemy to learning."[19]

Van believed that it is possible to make the academic entertaining; it is possible to have both laughter and learning at once with the right approach. Employing entertainment as a training strategy goes well beyond telling jokes and laughing. It is a powerful tool that can increase trainee engagement and ensure the retention of new concepts.

Even though Van came from a training background that had no relationship to Disneyland, his values and sense of humor aligned perfectly with Walt's. Tom Eastman, retired corporate director of the Disney University, provides a succinct description of Van that creates a vivid image: "Van was Disneyland's Jiminy Cricket, Disneyland's conscience, constantly emphasizing the importance of the Disneyland employees, the cast members. Van's great efforts were directed to the people side of our business." Tom adds, "Van was a happy rascal, an elf. He always had a great smile and a sparkle in his eye." This, combined with his dedication to the cast members, the guests, Disneyland, and the Disney values, proved to be a powerful combination.[20]

Walt Disney's values and sense of humor shaped Disneyland; Van's values and sense of humor helped shape the Disney University.

It Took More Than a Good Idea

Using Van's own words, "It took more than a good idea to bring the university into existence." And it took more than a good idea to ensure the success, longevity, and contributions of the Disney University.

Van France and his team of employee development pioneers brought to life the values found in the Four Circumstances. Disney corporate leadership along with Van and his team of strong-willed visionaries created a corporate culture and an organizational DNA well before those words were in vogue. They didn't just go to the store, buy pixie dust, and start throwing it around. Their tireless devotion to perpetuating Walt Disney's dream, plus the game-changing business concepts they created, helped build an organizational culture that is respected around the world.

Secrets of the Disney University

What does it take to create legions of amazingly motivated employees year after year? How does a training organization, or any organization for that matter, thrive well beyond the honeymoon period? The message from Van and the many who worked with him to create the Disney University is unwavering. Success is predicated on the following:

- Having a seat at the leadership table

- Being a valued part of the organizational culture

- Moving well beyond providing merely short-lived programs

- Being incessantly creative and willing to try new approaches to keep the message relevant, fresh, and engaging

The Four Circumstances reflect an organizational culture that has ensured for decades the survival of this new baby in the corporate family. The Four Circumstances also greatly influenced Van's leadership lessons, which are applicable to all organizations and are as relevant today as they were back then.

Setting the Stage for Success: The Four Circumstances of the Disney University

Beyond a University in Name Only

Van France identified the Four Circumstances, or components, that were vital to the success of the Disney University. They are:

1. **Innovate.** Leaders must be
   - Forward-thinking
   - Comfortable with risk

2. **Support.** Leaders must provide support that is
   - Overt
   - Enthusiastic
   - Sustained

3. **Educate.** Employee education and development must be
   - An indispensable component of organizational culture
   - Simple enough to remember and act upon
   - Implemented at all organizational levels

4. **Entertain.** Employee education and development must be
   - Engaging
   - Memorable
   - Fun

Walt's belief that laughter is no enemy to learning gave Van license to create training materials that transformed theory into action and the potentially boring into the memorable.

Applying Van's Four Circumstances

INNOVATE ● **SUPPORT** ● **EDUCATE** ● **ENTERTAIN**

What Are Your Circumstances?

Can you identify the equivalent of Van France's Four Circumstances in your organization? Do you apply them?

Identify: How do you set the stage for success to ensure sustained enthusiasm for employee development? What values in your organization are nonnegotiable? Identify them.

- Why are those values in place?
- What benefits do the values provide the organization and employees?
- Which values are the strongest? Which are the weakest?

Apply: How are the values of your organization brought to life?

- How are they communicated to employees? How often? By whom?
- Does everyone know the values?
- What happens when those values aren't upheld? Are there consequences? Are there exceptions? Are the consequences for following or not following the values consistent?
- How can the values be more effectively conveyed throughout your organization?

Capture Hearts and Minds

It's More Than Mickey Mouse
and Donald Duck

A maxim of the movie industry is that "it takes a happy crew to produce a happy show."[1]

—Van France

It is 1982. Dick Nunis, hoping to catch a quick cat nap, slumps into a chair at the back of the darkened room and closes his eyes. Exhausted and suffering from lack of sleep, he knows he has no option other than to press on. The five-minute run time of the video he just introduced to his audience will provide a much needed break. The grand opening of EPCOT Center, the $800 million expansion at Walt Disney World in Florida, is just around the corner, and he has much to do.

As president of the Outdoor Recreation Division for The Walt Disney Company, Dick is responsible for both Walt Disney World in Florida and Disneyland in California. With the 1982 EPCOT expansion project 11 years after the opening of the Magic Kingdom, Dick's responsibilities are vast, complicated, and expanding by the day.

Dick is the sole presenter of the employee orientation program for all EPCOT cast members. His audience isn't a select group of senior managers, nor is he merely the figure-head–executive–guest speaker brought in for a few minutes to kick off the session. Dick is giving this same 90-minute presentation to every cast member assigned to EPCOT—all 2,000 of them.

Today's session is similar to the dozens he has already conducted during the last week, and he must lead dozens more. When he is in front of his audience, Dick, in his in-imitable style, exudes energy and enthusiasm. He reaffirms with cast members the importance of maintaining the Dis-ney legacy of world-class guest service.

Twenty-seven years earlier, in preparation for the grand open-ing of Disneyland, Dick and his boss, Van France, kept up a similar frenetic pace. In fact, the content of these current sessions, as well as Dick's effusive style, isn't much different from what it was a quar-ter century earlier. At that time, he was fresh out of college and full of energy. Now, despite the never-ending demands on his time as a senior executive of The Walt Disney Company, Dick still sets the standard for enthusiasm and endurance. He is right in the middle of something he considers crucial to the success of EPCOT: guest service and cast member training.

As the video draws to a close, a staff member flicks on the room lights. Dick runs to the front of the room and contin-ues the orientation. The grand opening is just around the corner.

To prepare for the EPCOT grand opening, a brand new orien-tation program was designed for those who would be working at the park. To ensure the success of EPCOT, existing cast members were transferred from the Magic Kingdom. Although all were expe-rienced, Dick wanted them to fully understand their roles and their importance to this newest theme park, and so he conducted each and every session multiple times per day for two weeks.

Through his words and actions, Dick perpetuated the corporate culture he learned so many decades earlier from Walt Disney and Van France: "The Walt Disney Company cares about its employees and this project." By rolling up his sleeves and demonstrating his willingness to wear one of many hats, he reinforced Walt's and Van's belief that

- Management must be diligent or the *show* will deteriorate.

- Management must be diligent or the *cast* will deteriorate.[2]

The Disney University Is a Fun Place to Work

Working at the Disney University is a trainer's dream. Employees are happy to be there, both those who are providing the training and those who are receiving it. The images of world-famous cartoon characters grace the covers and pages of the training manuals. There is a catchy name for the new-hire orientation program—actually, for most of the programs. The walls are a whole other story. A constant reminder of the company's legacy and success are the posters, pictures, and artwork from Academy Award–winning movies and Tony Award–winning Broadway plays lining the walls of the hallways and training rooms.

The picture of Walt Disney receiving the Academy Award for his 1937 animated classic *Snow White and the Seven Dwarfs* stands out. Even the grumpiest trainer or trainee can't hold back a smile when looking at the Oscar award that Walt is receiving. There is the single, standard-size Oscar statue that anyone would recognize. But this Oscar is not alone; there are seven miniature Oscar statuettes lined up right next to him. Then there is that ever-present background music from the same motion pictures, animated features, and Broadway musicals. Who wouldn't be motivated by this selection of Grammy Award–winning tunes? In addition, the Disney

University is situated in a place tens of millions of people pay to visit every year. Finally, what training staff in the world wouldn't love kicking off a program that has Mickey Mouse or Donald Duck joining them at the front of the room leading a cheer?

It's Hard Work

Many executives and training professionals are envious of the Disney University. People think Disney trainers have an advantage. Quite a few think that if they had all that famous stuff, their training programs would be equally well attended and everyone would be enthusiastic. The excuses and rationale for ineffective training programs flow like water: "If I had the staff and budget of a Disney University, life would be easy." "If I had that kind of training environment, with all those famous characters and cutesy things, I'd never have problems getting people to show up. Who wouldn't love that?" "Disney has decades of history on its side. If my company had the equivalent of Disney's brand and legacy, I wouldn't have to worry."

Yes and no.

A Provider of Values, Not Just Things

The benefits the Disney University staff enjoys are undeniable, but glitz alone won't last. The honeymoon will end, and then what? In fact, the Disney University is much, much more than all these things. Van France would say, "A maxim of the movie industry is that 'it takes a happy crew to produce a happy show.'" Something in addition to *things* is necessary. Taking this metaphor a step further, Van would argue that a movie set blessed with the best props and the most famous actors is doomed if the crew is unhappy and the director doesn't provide support and direction. Certainly, movie props are important, but these things can take one only so far; there are limits to the life span and attractiveness of things. The enduring success of the Disney University—and the Disney brand itself—

is due to much more than cartoon characters and award-winning background music. Creating The Happiest Place on Earth is a fine balance of values *and* things, along with a lot of hard work.

The Disney University has a set of crystal-clear values that are aligned with and fiercely supported by the company leadership.

Many organizations have invested huge sums of money and countless hours studying the Disney way of doing business. They have done an admirable job of analyzing and then mimicking Disney's strategies for creating, building, and opening facilities that have world-class potential. But how successful are those businesses, resorts, hospitals, and organizations (for-profit as well as not-for-profit) at maintaining what they've created? Many fail in this department for two reasons:

- They focus on the stuff, the things, without the bedrock of values.

- They don't fully consider long-term consequences, the effect of short-sighted decisions on long-term success.

Without the conscience of passionately accepted organizational values leading the way, it is far too easy to begin cutting corners. There is a price to pay when things and the bottom line become the main focus. There are no exceptions to this rule.

Pulling Back the Curtain

According to Thor Degelmann, "Disney makes a complex operation look simple; therefore, everyone else thinks, 'I can do it.'" Thor's involvement in human resources and the Disney University for three of the company's most ambitious and complex projects—Walt Disney World in Florida, Tokyo Disneyland in Japan, and Disneyland Paris in France—gave him a front row seat for the many challenges. These projects cover a good portion of Thor's 32-year career at

Disney, but the message is the same: Disney's organizational values drive the strategies, which in turn drive Disney's success.

"The Disney University is the conscience of the organizational culture," says Thor. "Somebody always has to be the conscience. But it's not the university alone. The team in operations is equally involved. The key is that everyone in management buys into Walt Disney's message of 'keep the place clean, keep it friendly, and make it fun.' This culture drives the investment in our people."[3]

Investment comes in a variety of forms. Unfortunately, too many organizations don't take it far enough; they impose limits that eventually undermine employees and customers alike. By way of example, Thor says, "We didn't make the mistake made by so many other corporations by limiting our orientation and training to people on the front line. Everyone participates in training, not just the ride operators or those who have direct contact with guests. So, from maintenance personnel and administrative assistants all the way to executives, there is full participation. There is corporate commitment to this approach to training, starting from the top down."

In essence, the Disney University makes certain that every employee is properly introduced to the company and understands the importance of the brand: Disney values, Disney history, and Disney traditions. This context further enriches the specific on-the-job training (OJT) sessions conducted by the operations team which employees attend immediately after orientation.

Remember Sophie? She learned during her Disney University orientation that it is important to know who you are and where you came from in order to move ahead. She also learned that her day of orientation with the Disney University trainers was the first of several days of training. Before allowing its employees to have any direct contact with guests, the Disney University has determined that it is necessary that each employee attend the orientation program followed by the operations OJT sessions.

It's Everyone's Job

What else would you expect to hear from a toe-the-corporate-line executive who spent the bulk of his career in the Disney University? What about someone who spent his whole 34-year career on the front lines, in operations? What would he say?

Ron Pogue, who started as a ticket taker at Disneyland's front gate and eventually rose to the position of Vice President of Disneyland International, describes a fundamental value that drives decisions: "Walt Disney's philosophy for success might sound simple: 'Quality will win out, give the public everything you can give them, keep the place as clean as you can, and keep it friendly.' However, executing this philosophy every day, year after year, is the real challenge." Ron's career was as long as Thor's, but Ron's expertise is on the operations side of the business.

Van France and the staff of the Disney University worked hand in hand with the operations team to convey Walt's philosophy to *all* the employees. In essence, they successfully created a way to pass the baton from the Disney University training team to those in operations. The whole team in operations believes in the value of education and training. As Ron explains, "Every one of our employees—our cast members—knew their role, whether working on-stage or backstage. The key was ensuring that management understood this philosophy and then knew how to translate that core belief to our cast members consistently." Everyone knows his or her role in keeping the parks friendly, well maintained, and efficiently operating. This way of doing business—also known as the Disney Philosophy and the Disney Way—involves a huge investment of time, training, and money that not many others are willing to make. At Disneyland, the Disney Philosophy is not just a nice thing to do but a *must* do.[4]

Ron's comments sound eerily familiar, don't they?

Organizational values are typically exposed in the form of property and people maintenance. The "operations guy" Ron Pogue's comments reflect an equal concern for maintaining the property, the things, and the people. At the same time, Thor Degelmann, the "human resources guy," stresses the importance of the training sequence: Disney University training must be combined with on-the-job training in operations to ensure that property and people are prepared and maintained.

Consider the mirror-image similarities between the comments made by these two career executives, one from the Disney University and one from Disney Operations. Both are singing from the same sheet of music; they share the same values. How many corporate leaders can demonstrate that this is happening in their organizations?

Capturing Hearts and Minds

There are plenty of training departments and organizational development teams throughout the world that have a world-class staff and facilities and ample budgets. Many have at their disposal highly educated curriculum design specialists and the latest audiovisual technologies. On a program design and implementation level, a good number of organizations are fully capable of creating actual and virtual classrooms in every state, province, region, or country in which they operate.

Despite the resources at their disposal, too many training departments struggle to provide an educational experience that survives beyond the walls of those classrooms or the pages of their training manuals. Also, too many training departments fail to get employees' support of the concepts, strategies, guidelines, rules, regulations, ideas, and procedures presented during training. To overcome these problems, the heads of organizations and training departments might start by addressing these questions:

- Why aren't the standard operating procedures of our company followed?

- Why is it so difficult to provide best-in-class customer service consistently?

- Why is it so hard to create and then sustain momentum?

Even the lowest-tech, bare-bones, and budget-challenged training program will get the job done as long as hearts and minds are captured. Training programs reflect organizational values and health. The content of training programs, the individuals who teach, the employees who attend, and the way employees are supported outside the classroom reveal much about organizational culture. Many organizations would benefit by simply looking at what their training activities (or lack of training activities) are telling them. Which of Van France's Four Circumstances are present? Combined, they ensure that hearts and minds are engaged.

- Is *innovation* encouraged? To what extent is creative out-of-the-box thinking fostered both in the training environment and on the job?

- Is *organizational support* found at every level? Are leaders, from C-level executives to front-line supervisors, aligned with the training team? Is their support overt and enthusiastic? Do operations staff and training staff collaborate to ensure the effectiveness of content and delivery methods?

- Is employee *education* valued and nonnegotiable? Or is training the first thing that is cut when budgets are tight? (If Van France's second circumstance—organizational support—is truly in place, training doesn't get cut.)

- Is *entertainment* incorporated into training and education initiatives? Is training engaging and practical? Are experiential training techniques that have enough shock value (simulations, role-plays, exercises) employed to get maximum involvement from all trainees, even the introverts? When it is used effectively, entertainment has a place in virtually any training environment; it helps transform theory into action and the boring into the memorable.

The image of Dick Nunis personally conducting dozens of orientation programs, enough to reach thousands of cast members, sends a powerful message. Indeed, having the president of any company preside over employee orientation or training is unusual, and this is most likely a stretch for the majority of leaders. Yet the exact opposite is too often the case: disconnected and distant executives sending messages of indifference through their lack of involvement and support.

The Disney University's success is due to its uncanny ability to capture the hearts and minds of the thousands of employees it serves. Van France blended his values with those of Walt Disney, Dick Nunis, and a cast of brilliantly creative leaders. He then turned them into a groundbreaking approach to employee development. To this day, decades after its founding, the Disney University continues to produce results envied by business leaders around the world.

The Disney University is certainly a lot more than Mickey Mouse and Donald Duck.

Capture Hearts and Minds: It's More Than Mickey Mouse and Donald Duck

Providing Values, Not Just Things

- *Things* have a limited shelf life. The strength and durability of the Disney University message transcends the fame of the Disney characters and products.

- Values bring to life both the lowest-tech and highest-tech training methods.

- The Disney University represents the values of the company.

Pulling Back the Curtain

- Disney University's training goals and content are aligned with and supported by those in the field, the operations team.

- The Disney Philosophy drives every decision both in operations and in the Disney University.

It's Everyone's Job

- Organizational values are exposed in the form of property and people maintenance.

- Management must be diligent or the show will deteriorate. Management must be diligent or the cast will deteriorate.

Applying Van's Four Circumstances

INNOVATE ● **SUPPORT** ● **EDUCATE** ● **ENTERTAIN**

Capture Hearts and Minds

In your organization, can you identify the equivalent of Van's Four Circumstances that support highly trained, well-prepared, and motivated employees? How do you apply those circumstances to capture employees' hearts and minds?

How Does Your Organization Balance Values and Things?

- What is your equivalent of Mickey Mouse or Donald Duck, your claim to fame? Perhaps it is your technology, your award-winning products, or your world-class distribution channels.

- How do you balance these things with values?

Pulling Back the Curtain

- Are training goals aligned with corporate goals?

- Are all your divisions and business units (legal, marketing, operations, production, finance, etc.) engaged in your training efforts? If so, how can those bonds be strengthened? If not, what is missing?

It's Everyone's Job (Starting at the Top)

- Does your leadership team demonstrate unwavering support of employee development and training efforts? Is there a culture of learning and training?

- Who promotes your organizational culture? Who is your equivalent of Walt Disney, Van France, or Dick Nunis (arguably, role models of excellence for aspiring chief cultural officers)?

It Takes Art and Science

The Attractions Don't Break Down, and Snow White Never Has a Bad Day

To try to keep an operation like Disneyland going you have to pour it [money] in there. It's not just new attractions, but keeping it staffed properly, you know . . . never letting your personnel get sloppy. Never let them be unfriendly.[1]

—**Walt Disney**

Walt Disney got off the Jungle Cruise boat and wasn't happy. In fact, something was terribly wrong. The problem was with the skipper of the boat Walt had observed. The skipper hadn't done his job properly, and that simply wasn't acceptable to Walt. Yes, the skipper ran the boat safely, so that wasn't the problem. Yes, he had recited his script line for line, so that wasn't the problem. It was something else. It was in his delivery; he hadn't acted his part with as much enthusiasm as Walt wanted. He lacked energy and showmanship.

Ron Dominguez, who retired as executive vice president of Walt Disney Attractions, was the supervisor of the area where Jungle

Cruise is situated. "We got word that Walt was furious that he got a lousy spiel on Jungle Cruise, and he let my boss, Dick Nunis, know just how upset he was," Ron explained.

"Walt told Dick, 'I want the skippers to act as if every trip on the Jungle Cruise is their first trip. I want them to act surprised when the hippos suddenly rise out of the water. The skippers need to be as surprised as the guests.'"

At that point, Dick, Ron, and the whole Jungle Cruise team started a marathon training program to ensure that all the employees knew the script and performed their roles with the appropriate enthusiasm.

Ron went on to explain that he and Dick Nunis "immediately began assessing the spiel of each skipper. We rode with each of them. After the ride was over, we sat on the Jungle Cruise dock and critiqued their performances, specifically, their enthusiasm. Walt had a tendency of popping in unannounced on Sunday afternoons, so we were determined to be up to speed by the time of his next visit. Walt's message to us was, 'The best is never the best, and pay attention to the smallest details.'"[2]

Balancing Art and Science

Walt Disney and Van France knew the importance of achieving and maintaining a balance of art and science. Building and maintaining Disneyland—the attractions, restaurants, shops, and arcades—is just the starting point: the science. Maintaining the feel of Disneyland and employee morale is the art. Combined, they create a powerful differentiator from the competition: the stores, restaurants, resorts, and amusement parks vying for the same customers and employees. Van, Walt's equal at being a taskmaster, incessantly promoted the art of friendliness. Walt and Van, the cheerleaders for balance, wouldn't tolerate Disneyland falling into the trap plaguing so many of its competitors:

- *Keep the park clean.* The competition isn't as focused on cleanliness. Their rides are dirty, and the grounds are full of litter. Their employees' uniforms are wrinkled or stained.

- *Keep the park well maintained.* The competition may have faster rides, but they aren't well maintained and frequently break down.

- *Keep the park friendly.* The competition may have plenty of employees, but they aren't well trained; they don't know the answers to customers' questions, plus they aren't as friendly.

Walt's ride on the Jungle Cruise, along with his scathing comment, is a clear example of his focus on the upkeep of the park and the importance of maintaining both the art and the science of the show: never let the rides suffer from a lack of proper care, keep the property clean, and keep it friendly.[3] Cast members and leaders at Disney properties refer to this process as keeping the property and show fresh.

Keep the Park Fresh

The term *fresh* encompasses Walt's strategy for keeping Disneyland relevant and competitive, the never-ending pursuit of perfection. Walt's philosophy of keeping the park clean, fresh, and friendly extends to every cast member and every attraction. Timely upkeep of attractions keeps them fresh. Continuous development of cast members keeps them fresh, engaged, and enthusiastic.

Ten years after Disneyland opened, Walt reinforced his commitment to keeping Disneyland fresh. During the tenth anniversary celebration, Walt thanked his pioneering group of imagineers and staff for their hard work in making Disneyland successful. However, he closed the evening with this comment:

I just want to leave you with this thought, that it's just been sort of a dress rehearsal and we're just getting started. So, if any of you start to rest on your laurels, I mean, just forget it.[4]

Disneyland was a decade into an unprecedented run of success, and Walt referred to it as a "dress rehearsal." Walt's admonition to his leaders to avoid resting on their laurels underscores the need for constant improvement and attention to the details. Resting on one's laurels is the equivalent of getting stale, a condition not acceptable to Walt. He expected the exact opposite: keep Disneyland fresh by constantly maintaining the property, keeping it clean, updating attractions, and ensuring that every cast member receives world-class training.

Sharing the Stage

From its inception in 1955, Walt, Van, and the leadership team knew that the unique environment of Disneyland would pose new challenges to the company. For the first time in the history of Walt Disney Productions, the audience and the actors would be sharing the stage, with the show constantly evolving. Until Disneyland came along, the team at the Disney Studios worked solely in film production. As Walt Disney says:

A picture is a thing, once you wrap it up and turn it over to Technicolor [film labs], you're through.[5]

Not in the Disneyland environment. Unlike a conventional theater, where the distance between the audience and the entertainers on stage doesn't allow for close inspection, at Disneyland those being entertained would be in direct contact with the entertainers. In effect, not only were the guests invited to join the entertainers onstage, they were allowed to closely inspect both the actors and the set. This did not allow for cheaply built stage props, shabby Disney character costumes, and heavily made-up entertainers.

The new entertainment environment of Disneyland also brought forth the question, just *who* are the "entertainers"? Van and his initial team of trainers wanted everyone to understand that "when you're on-stage, you're an entertainer," a term not limited to those in direct contact with guests such as those parking cars, serving food, operating attractions, and performing as the famous Disney characters. It would also include maintenance personnel, the grounds crew, and the custodial cast members, who during operating hours would be scrutinized by guests and therefore were as much a part of the show as were the others. This unique environment creates unprecedented challenges and opportunities for many cast members to perform two jobs at once:

- Maintenance and grounds crew cast members are trained to extend a helping hand to lost guests.

- Custodial cast members (sweepers) learn that taking pictures of families leaves a lasting and positive impression.

- Security cast members know the power of addressing a child by name.

The Disney University staff constantly reinforces the message that cast members perform multiple roles such as in the following example:

Leslie, a security cast member, spots a child, bends down, and asks, "Hi, Jamal. Are you having fun today?" This brief interaction creates a moment neither child nor parent will ever forget. How do they know the child's name? *(Hint: Cast members are constantly on the lookout for children wearing Mickey Mouse ears caps. The children's names are usually embroidered on the front of the cap.)*

"We Want to Meet Snow White"

One of the first lessons learned by all cast members is, "Disneyland itself is the star; everything else is in the supporting role."[6] In other words, no divas allowed. A cast packed with potent supporting-role talent can be responsible for the success of a production, but the converse is equally true: An actor cast in a supporting role (not the lead) can destroy a play created by the world's best designers, producers, scriptwriters, and construction crews. An off-key singer in a seemingly insignificant role can distract the audience from the beauty of the set and the skills of the other actors. At Disneyland, all cast members know that regardless of their role, they can make or break the guests' experience.

No one knows who originally came up with the following story—a powerful and fictional one—that Disney University trainers relate during orientation, but it has Van's fingerprints all over it. The image it creates in the mind of every cast member is potent, unambiguous, and everlasting.

> Pretend just for a moment that a family of five has just passed through the main entrance at Disneyland or Walt Disney World. They have been traveling for hours by car, bus, or airplane, and Mom and Dad are exhausted; the three kids are beyond excited. In fact, the kids have been amped up for the last three months, ever since they learned of their Disney vacation. They have been talking nonstop, saying, "We can't wait to meet Snow White to get her autograph and photograph."

> Fast-forward 30 minutes. Now everyone is finally in the park.

> Mom and Dad are having their first cup of coffee, and the kids are scrambling around, looking for Snow White. Then they see her! She looks as beautiful as they had imagined.

The kids rush toward Snow White for her autograph—they will get it! Surrounding Snow White, the kids are all pulling on her cape and screaming, "We want your autograph," "We want your autograph!"

Let's take it to the next step.

Pretend Snow White is fed up with their noise and is having a bad day. She had a tough commute this morning, and the Seven Dwarfs are late to work. Snow White is in a foul, foul mood. In a fit of rage, she spins around, glares at the kids, and barks, "Leave me alone. Can't you see that I don't want to be bothered?" To make things even worse, Snow White has a cigarette dangling from her mouth. Her wig is pushed way back on her head, and her dress is wrinkled and dirty.

At this point, what is the effect on the kids? Are they still thrilled to be at Disneyland? Do you think Mom and Dad, watching this scene from a distance, are saying to each other, "Gee, isn't it great that Disney keeps this place so clean? I heard that a virtual army of employees comes out every night to fix the rides and scrub away dirt, fingerprints, and clumps of gooey gum on the ground. I love this place." Is this what they are saying to each other?

Of course, newly hired cast members always get a good laugh out of this story. At first it sounds like a ridiculous scenario. Could anyone ever imagine Snow White being so rude or looking like such a slob? What about cast members in more supporting roles working in the parking lot, the restaurants, or the retail stores? They too, with a frown or caustic tone, can ruin a guest's day, much the way one off-key supporting-role singer can detract viewers from the otherwise flawless execution of a musical.

The Disney University staff then asks orientation participants to think of other scenarios in which they themselves have been the customer, patient, or client. It is always an eye-opener for trainees to find out from one another how often they come into contact with service providers who are as inattentive or rude as our imaginary Snow White.

Know the Job and Do It with a Smile

Even the most recent graduates of Disney University training know the importance of art and science. Friendliness and technical competence are a formidable combination. For the cast member playing Snow White, this means two things:

- *The art of being Snow White.* She receives extensive training about how to handle the reality of performing while surrounded by the audience. Snow White knows she will have to interact with guests of all ages *and* be friendly. Her *interpersonal expertise* ensures that she won't view these interactions with guests as bothersome interruptions.

- *The science of being Snow White.* She has to *become* Snow White. She has to know every movement portrayed by Snow White in the classic movie. Her *technical expertise* helps transform her into the character.

Far too many organizations have difficulty attaining this balance of friendliness and technical competence. The process of developing employees who know the job and can do it with a smile escapes too many corporate training departments. Companies that tolerate technically competent but rude employees (or indifferent employees) will suffer. Of course, smiling employees can't make up for an outdated product line or flawed technology. Putting all one's eggs in either the science or the art basket will eventually drive away the people who really matter: good employees and valued customers.

Walt's message to the Jungle Cruise crew was clear: The advanced technology and well-maintained operating system that makes the attraction so compelling is just part of a complex puzzle. The lifelike lions and hippos, the compelling sound track, and the tropical plants fill in part of the puzzle. The boat, expertly painted to make it appear old and rusty, is another piece. So too is the clean safari-themed costume provided to the skipper. Finally, the skipper's enthusiastic delivery of the scripted spiel completes the picture. All these interlocking pieces when combined deliver an enchanting experience to the guest. This adventure can be undermined instantly by an unenthusiastic cast member. The Disney University keeps Walt's and Van's message alive. Amazing things happen when art and science are given equal billing: attractions operate consistently, and Snow White has only good days.

It Takes Art and Science:
The Attractions Don't Break Down, and
Snow White Never Has a Bad Day

Balance Art and Science

- The combination of friendliness (*art*) and a compelling product or service (*science*) is a powerful competitive differentiator. Neither art nor science alone is sufficient.

- Know the job (science) and do it with a smile (art). The equivalent of a surly Snow White or an unenthusiastic Jungle Cruise skipper can undermine a whole organization.

- Even the most enthusiastic Jungle Cruise skippers are doomed to fail if their boats keep breaking down.

Keep the Park Fresh

"It's just been sort of a dress rehearsal, and we're just getting started."

Walt Disney's message to his leadership team at Disneyland, even after a decade of success, is clear: becoming stale isn't an option.

- The best is never the best.

- Constantly upgrading and maintaining the property and attractions is only the beginning.

- Ensuring that the staff is educated and enthusiastic is equally important.

Applying Van's Four Circumstances

INNOVATE ● **SUPPORT** ● **EDUCATE** ● **ENTERTAIN**

How do you apply Van France's Four Circumstances in your organization? How do you apply them to the key areas identified in this lesson: balancing art and science and keeping the park fresh? Which of the Four Circumstances are the strongest? Which are the weakest?

Balance Art and Science

Is there an equivalent to a cranky Snow White, an unenthusiastic Jungle Cruise skipper, or a broken-down Jungle Cruise boat in your organization?

- If so, why is this tolerated?
- What needs to be done to change this environment?
- What are the barriers?
- Who in your organization can lead the way?

Keep the Park Fresh

- How do you upgrade your product, service, property, and staff to keep everything fresh?
- Where could you make improvements?
- What will it cost to improve?
- What will it cost not to improve?

Gather Facts and Feelings

Walk the Park

Walt would regularly walk through the Park, looking for problems or things to improve. He was good at it and always welcomed suggestions. I copied his routine. I continually walked through the Park, looking for different things, people problems. Facts are easy to identify, I was looking for feelings that were bothering Cast Members.[1]

—**Van France**

Van, with camera in hand, sets out from his office, a ramshackle hut in the backstage area of Disneyland. As usual, he is going into the park.

He doesn't have a particular schedule, but his agenda is always the same: connect with and interact with as many guests and cast members as possible.

He passes through a gate marked "For Cast Members Only" in Fantasyland and enters the on-stage area of Disneyland. Thousands of guests are scampering about, intent on getting the most out of their day. Adjusting the shutter on his camera, Van starts clicking away. He knows this handy little tool is an instant bridge, a nonthreatening way to help initiate contact with guests and cast members. After all, who would turn down the opportunity to have his or her picture taken at Disneyland? Guests love it, and cast members are always game for hamming it up.

Today, Van glides through the park, from Fantasyland to Tomorrowland and then Main Street, comfortably engaging guests and cast members . . . and taking pictures. He moves between on-stage and backstage areas of Disneyland.

"How is your day going?" he asks a cast member in first aid who is helping a toddler with a scraped knee. "Can I take your picture?"

Click.

Approaching a newlywed couple in front of Sleeping Beauty Castle, camera in hand and with a big smile, Van asks, "Are you having fun at Disneyland today?"

Click.

He knows guests always love gathering for a photo. At the Submarine Voyage he spots a family of five: "Let's get the whole family in this picture."

Click.

At the Disneyland main entrance, Van works the turn-stiles, checking guests' tickets and cracking jokes. He engages elderly guests with the question, "Can I see your ID, please?"

He talks with the on-stage cast members responsible for running attractions, serving food, and selling merchandise. Van wants diverse opinions from a variety of sources, and so he takes time to chat with the sweepers and the custodial crews. After all, who knows more about the condition of the park than those in maintenance?

He spends over half his time backstage, interacting with the cast members who are supporting the show. One moment, Van chats with the kitchen host at the Inn Between, the Disneyland employee cafeteria situated directly behind the Plaza Inn restaurant. The host is busily stirring a massive pot of chili. Next, Van is in an employee break area and engages several cast members who are eating sandwiches.

Returning to his backstage office, Van puts down the camera and settles in behind his desk. While inserting a piece of paper into his typewriter, he thinks about the many comments he gathered during his walk through the park. Many are positive, but some are critical and require action.

Although Van's data-gathering process is far from scientific, it does the job. Even though his name badge identifies him as an employee, the combination of his camera, quick wit, and ready smile helps guests and cast members relax; they don't hesitate to open up and share their opinions.

Van, a prolific writer, starts pounding away at the typewriter keys. His focus shifts to his camera, and he smiles. It has served him well. Today it was loaded with film, but last week . . .

A Different Perspective

Walt Disney knew the value of learning as much as possible about the front lines by spending time *on* the front lines.

From his apartment above the Fire Station at Disneyland, Walt would venture into the park at all hours to interact with guests and cast members. Ron Miller, former CEO of Walt Disney Productions—and Walt Disney's son-in-law—spent time with his family and Walt in that very apartment and knows the pattern well: "Walt cared about everyone. He would come out of his apartment at night just to interact with the maintenance crew, with the guys sweeping the dust out of the trolley tracks on Main Street."[2]

Walt's strategy of walking the park dates back to the construction phase of Disneyland. He regularly visited the construction site to assess the proportion or size of buildings. A common sight was

Walt squatting down and then looking up at a building from a lower angle. Walt's equally common comment "Can you see little kids looking up at this?" kept his planners and designers on their toes. Walt's determination to view the storefronts and buildings from the vantage point of children ensured that the needs of this large population of guests—an often overlooked group—were addressed.[3]

Walt Disney never stopped looking at Disneyland from the perspective of the guest, even years after the park opened. Cast members couldn't predict the unexpected moment when Walt would appear.

> The Fantasyland ride operator is busily moving the Skyway gondolas through the loading area. It is midwinter, and there aren't many guests at Disneyland, nor on his attraction. He turns briefly and is startled to see Walt Disney sitting on a bench watching him.
>
> Walt calls out, "Can I talk to you for a minute?"
>
> "Yes, sir," says the cast member, as he nervously makes his way to the bench to sit next to Walt. While he has heard about these moments when Walt would unexpectedly emerge, this is a first for him.
>
> "We're thinking of updating the skyway," Walt informs him. "You work on this attraction every day, so I can't think of anyone more qualified to give me ideas for the new design."
>
> A bit surprised, the cast member considers Walt's comment, and then offers his suggestion. "Actually, the gondola roofs are too low and guests often bump their heads when I load and unload them."
>
> When they finished this brief exchange of ideas, Walt thanked him. Intending to get a closer look at the attraction, Walt proceeded to board one of the gondolas . . . and he bumped his head!

Recalling that day, the cast member says, "Walt took the time to ask me, an 18-year-old cast member, for my opinion about the

Skyway." Even more impressive is the fact that the newly redesigned Skyway had gondolas with higher roofs.[4]

Van, like Walt, favored walking the park to gather information. Often armed with his trusty camera (with or without film), Van tirelessly sought the opinions and thoughts of cast members and guests.[5] He was a master at connecting with and reading people.[6] From his first days on the job until the day he retired, Van maintained contact with guests, hourly paid cast members, executives, and everyone in between. Their perspectives provided Van with fresh points of view; walking the park gave Van new insights.

Bill Ross spent countless hours with Van during his 32-year career at The Walt Disney Company. Before retiring as senior vice president of public affairs, Bill managed the Disney University and says, "More than anyone I've ever known, Van put his ear to the ground to get ideas. He had a wide circle of friends and a strong network. If Van were with us today, he would love using social media networks."[7]

Van's ability to gather facts *and* feelings proved invaluable when Disneyland faced a critical period of development.

Disneyland and Van Evolve

The idea for creating the Disney University, as it is known today, started in 1962. Seven years after the 1955 grand opening of Disneyland, the park had grown and changed in a variety of ways, from the number and complexity of attractions to the expanding employee population. Along with that expansion came the inevitable growing pains. Deteriorating employee morale and the haphazard (at times nonexistent) approach to employee training were the most troubling to Van.

Van also had changed since his initial years working with Walt and the original Disneyland leadership team. After creating the revolutionary orientation program that would "mold a group of diverse Californians with no business experience into producers of the 'Disneyland Dream,'" Van briefly left the company. His work external to Disney took him from designing orientation and training programs for other recreation-oriented organizations to advising urban planners on matters that included improving city design. Now, two years later, Van was back at Disneyland. His absence from the park had given him a fresh perspective, and he was eager to launch new approaches.

The Seven-Year Itch

Van likened Disneyland's challenges to the seven-year itch that can affect marriages. Perhaps it was more like the infant in the terrible twos stage or the teenager who rejects authority. Whatever the label, it first started at Disneyland in the early 1960s. The Happiest Place on Earth was seven years old and began experiencing some employee morale problems.[8] Determined to ferret out the core issues, Van employed a strategy he had used years earlier when he worked as a trainer in an airplane factory: he got out and "walked the factory floor" at Disneyland.

That opened his eyes to some underlying problems. As Van describes it, "There was a definite reality gap between the romance we preached in orientation and the actualities of some jobs."[9] The orientation program he and Dick Nunis originated in 1955 needed to be upgraded. He also discovered growing friction between the employees in some departments. Operations and maintenance crews shared a mutual antagonism about their respective value. Van knew that sustaining the magic of Disneyland would be impossible as long as maintenance employees called operations employees (those who ran the attractions) "button pushers" and operations employees called those in maintenance "bulb changers."

Van also learned that the leadership style of some managers greatly frustrated a number of cast members. Essentially, the autocratic leadership style from the post–World War II era through the

1950s wasn't working with the younger cast members.[10] The new generation demanded a more inclusive style of leadership.

Van continued to walk the park and gather data, interacting with cast members at all levels. His unique ability to connect with the front lines was enhanced by his ability to gather both facts and feelings. Van says, "Facts are easy to identify. I was looking for feelings that were bothering cast members. I would never turn people off when they wanted to gripe or blow off steam."[11]

One Foot in the Past, One Foot in the Future

Walking the park helped Van clarify the problems and then visualize a process by which to bridge the gaps. In spite of his emotional connection to the original orientation program he and Dick Nunis had created, Van recognized the urgency for change.

Van's and Dick's 1955-era orientation program, "We Create Happiness" coupled with the training provided by those in operations meant that a newly hired cast member could literally be operating an attraction within hours of joining the company. A common pattern of this original training process was as follows:

- New cast member is hired.

- Cast member *may* attend new-hire orientation (the administration of this was sporadic).

- Cast member, unescorted, finds the costuming department.

- Cast member, unescorted, finds way to assigned work area.

- Cast member receives overview of the operations from senior cast member.

- Cast member begins work shift.

This approach worked during the initial years of Disneyland's operations, when the park was smaller, operations were less complex, and there were fewer people to train. Without a doubt, those dedicated teams of cast members from the initial years of park operations provided an outstanding product. But with the growth of Disneyland came increased complexity, and the employee training process had to evolve.

The 1955 model of orientation and cast member training that had been so successful during Disneyland's early years was no longer sufficient. Van faced a paradox: preserving the past while preparing for the future. He needed to identify and preserve the components of orientation and training that had led to such heady success during Disneyland's first seven years:

- Friendly environment

- Creative presentations

- Useful content.

He had to balance these fundamentals while preparing cast members—including managers—for a much more complex future, driven by the following factors:

- *Consistency.* Everyone must attend the new-hire orientation program.

- *Systems.* Specific on-the-job training must follow the orientation program.

- *Continuing education.* Supervisors and managers needed leadership and communication-skills training.

Marty Sklar, who retired after a 50-year career from The Walt Disney Company as vice chairman of Walt Disney Imagineering, says this of Van: "Van enthusiastically carried out standards originally put in place by Walt Disney. Plus, Van's experience outside the world of show business was a big plus; he saw things differently."

Marty, who also worked directly with Walt on a number of projects, knows the pressure Van must have been feeling to improve training while respecting the company legacy. Walt constantly dealt with similar pressure and was a good role model for his young executives.

According to Marty, "Walt had one foot in the past and one foot in the future. He didn't make our company's history the most important thing, but he kept it alive. He used the history as a foundation from which he built a bridge to the future."[12]

The time was right for Van to build a bridge to the future of training for Disneyland. The time was right for the Disney University.

Gather Facts and Feelings
Walk the Park

A Fresh Perspective

- During his entire career, Van maintained contact with guests, cast members, executives, and everyone in between.

- Like Walt, Van regularly walked the park, looking for problems or things to improve.

The Happiest Place on Earth?

- Disneyland evolved in the first seven years of operation into a larger, more complex environment.

- The training of cast members hadn't evolved with the park, and employee morale started to suffer.

- Van identified a reality gap between the romance preached in orientation and the reality of life on the front line.

- Younger cast members rejected the autocratic leadership styles that had been prevalent in the 1940s and 1950s.

Gather Facts and Feelings

- Facts are easy to identify. Van looked for feelings that were bothering cast members.

- Van never rejected people who needed to gripe or blow off steam.

One Foot in the Past, One Foot in the Future

- Balance organizational history and legacy with current and future needs.

- Organizational history isn't the most important thing. Preserve history and use it as a foundation for building bridges to the future.

Applying Van's Four Circumstances

INNOVATE ● **SUPPORT** ● **EDUCATE** ● **ENTERTAIN**

Gather Facts and Feelings

In your organization, can you identify the equivalent of Van's Four Circumstances that support walking the park and keeping in touch with the front lines? How do you apply those circumstances to gather facts and feelings from employees and customers?

Walk the Park

- What is the equivalent of walking the park in your organization? Who does it and how frequently?

- How could this strategy be improved? More people involved? Greater frequency?

- If leaders aren't walking the park, what is the excuse?

- Walt Disney could carve time out of his day to walk the park. Why can't every leader do that?

The Happiest Place on Earth?

- Is there a reality gap between the ideals espoused in your orientation and training programs and the realities of the job?

- How is the effectiveness of training assessed? With what frequency?

One Foot in the Past, One Foot in the Future

- How is the history of your organization kept alive? How could this be improved?

- How does your organization balance history and legacy with current and future needs? Who supports this?

Be Willing to Change or Be Willing to Perish

The Birth of the Disney University

Our theme of "happiness" was great for the first years, and we still use basic elements of that program. But now we needed something new, something that would impose responsibility and self-discipline on all of our key people.[1]

—Van France

It is the fall of 1962, and Jim, recently mustered out of the army and studying at a local college, is walking through Disneyland on his way to work. His job as a foreman on the Matterhorn has his head spinning with possibilities. Deep in thought, he barely notices the weight of the stack of books under his arm—books he plans on using to prepare for an upcoming project. Jim is determined to improve the employee training process at the Matterhorn.

He contemplates the existing approach used for training the operators. It is a word-of-mouth process from the older guys to the younger guys. This method has worked for years, but the park is growing, and so is the number of employees. The training process also needs to evolve.

Influenced by his exposure to training in the Army, Jim is working on a standardized training program that will ensure the accuracy and consistency of information shared with all Matterhorn operators.

Out of the corner of his eye he spots Walt Disney walking through the park, hands in pockets. Walt is coming toward him. It is a Saturday morning, and Jim, as well as every other Disneyland employee, knows that Walt likes to walk the park on weekends. Jim, flustered, tries to avoid eye contact. It doesn't work.

Walt calls out, "Hey, Jim, come over here."

How does Walt know my name? Jim wonders. Caught up in the moment, Jim forgets that his name is clearly written on the brass name badge he is wearing.

"That's a lot of books," Walt says. "What are you studying?"

"I'm a college student," Jim replies. He adds, "Plus I'm working on a new Matterhorn operator training program. I just got out of the Army, and I think we could benefit from implementing a training process similar to what I experienced there. We could use a training program that has consistency and checklists to ensure accuracy."

Listening intently, Walt responds, "I was in the Army during World War I, and that kind of training makes sense to me."

Walt then adds a comment that Jim will never forget: "There's a guy over in administration named Van France who you might like to meet. Van is starting something called the University of Disneyland. If you're interested in doing training, go meet Van and tell him Walt sent you."[2]

More Than a University in Name Only

The Disney University was created seven years after the grand opening of Disneyland in response to the demands of a rapidly maturing organization. Despite the success of Van's original model for employee orientation, it was time to evolve and improve.

Walking the park and interacting with the large number of cast members exposed Van to the inadequacies of the existing orientation and training process—or complete lack thereof. He could see the reasons some of the more senior cast members derided the happiness theme of orientation as nothing more than a bunch of superficial "pixie dust."

- The training material was dated.

- The presenters were out of touch with the realities of park operations.

- Jobs that had started out as temporary summer work became careers.

- Working long hours on weekends, nights, and holidays was hard work.

- Cast members were exhausted and were becoming jaded.

Van also saw the need to expand beyond the simple orientation program of 1955 into a more complete sequence that included a consistently applied on-the-job training component. Finally, the supervisors and managers needed exposure to contemporary communications and leadership skills.

Of greatest concern to Van was credibility. He says, "'The University' was a good name, but would it have any substance in the organization?"[3]

Applicable Content, Credible Delivery

Determined to redesign the orientation and training program, Van had to distance himself from the past—as special as it had been—to ensure the future not only of training but of Disneyland itself.

Although Van didn't have a staff of full-time trainers in the early days of the Disney University, he didn't let that deter him from creating and presenting a world-class orientation program for the new employees of Disneyland. He began actively recruiting for the Disney University by looking for, as he describes it, "a unique crew of young people who were out there actually working the attractions and who shared Walt's dream."[4]

Jim, that young Matterhorn supervisor, was one of four operations guys who, along with Van, started the Disney University in 1963. Those young operators brought to the university a wealth of practical experience and had credibility with cast members.

Jim says, "In addition to my job in operations, I conducted new-hire orientation programs in the university for about 16 hours per week. I realized that in order to be a better trainer, I needed to learn more about the jobs my trainees would be performing once they left the university. I would go to the other divisions and learn everything about their jobs."[5]

Walking the park reinforced in Van's mind the requisite elements for ensuring "substance" in the Disney University:

• Training staff had to have credibility.

• Trainers with frontline experience were a must.

• Program content had to reflect the reality of the workplace and still convey corporate values, standards, and expectations.

Van knew that the practical experience of his new team of trainers, whether from attractions, food and beverage, maintenance, merchandise, or security, would serve as a vital credibility bridge to the many cast members who had become jaded. Their experience, coupled with a training curriculum that was believable, would make the difference.

Experienced as they were in operations, these new members of Van's Disney University team were not ready for the classroom. Jim adds, "We all worked in other areas of the park, so we knew the operations side of the business, but we weren't professional trainers. So Van developed a program called Laboratory of Communications Skills. He taught us all how to give presentations that were entertaining and informative."[6]

Van's ability to train others, combined with his strategy of staffing the Disney University with, as he says, "young kids who had enthusiasm and experience working in operations,"[7] proved a powerful combination.

Beyond Orientation

Dave Smith, chief archivist emeritus of Walt Disney Archives, says, "Van argued that the university should be a pioneering force, the world's first and foremost corporate institution for training in the arts, skills, and knowledge required in outdoor show business."

According to Van, "One basic goal of our university was to make working at Disneyland a new profession, a respected branch of show business."[8] With this in mind, Van proposed that the Disney University develop employees into "Disneyland specialists," with emphasis on four areas[9]:

Leaders: "We need to develop leaders who have an overall understanding of the complex combination of skills and professions that have made the Disneyland show the world's greatest entertainment attraction."

People specialists: "We need men and women who are professionally qualified to deal with people and their many demands."

Trade specialists: "We need to develop those skilled in the various unique technical phases of the operation, but they must also have an overall knowledge of the total operation."

History and traditions: "Most importantly, we sorely need training in the Disneyland organization and the history and traditions of Walt and his company."

Disney University:
Where Everyone Majors in "People"

The success of the Disney University is due to a number of factors, most important, Van's Four Circumstances, first introduced in Lesson 1 and repeated in each Lesson Review. However, there is another factor that plays a crucial role in its success and one that other training organizations would do well to emulate; its purpose is crystal clear. A statement in a 1969 university catalog outlining course offerings sums it up:

> *Whether you are a new host or hostess, starting out on your first job or an experienced old-timer, the University of Disneyland was established to assist you. It is an educational facility where everyone majors in "people." Our ability to deal with people in a personal and courteous way is the basis for our success.*[10]

Disney University:
Tradition and Innovation

The death of Walt Disney in 1966 presented Van and his team with a most daunting challenge: filling the void left by Walt. Roy Disney, who was determined to maintain the standards set by Walt, asked Van to prepare a new generation of orientation materials.

Van, with assistance from his Disney University team and numerous others, ultimately created a booklet called *The Walt Disney*

Traditions at Disneyland.[11] Van knew that Walt's passing "made it more important than ever for the University to create programs which would carry on the traditions, philosophies and dreams which he left for the organization."[12]

The *Traditions* booklet formed the basis for the Disney University's venerable Traditions orientation program, variations of which are still presented in every Disney University in the world.

Over the years, the Disney University continued evolving in response to a constantly shifting environment. From the passing of Walt Disney to the employee strike and corporate leadership changes of the mid-1980s and beyond, the leadership and staff of the Disney University has steadfastly followed Van's admonition to change or perish.

Van's vision of ensuring that the university "would have substance in the organization" created the blueprint for balancing tradition and innovation. Emblematic is a story from the late 1970s. Van, energized after a round of walking the park and engaging cast members, vaults into action:

> Van walks into the Disney University manager's office, sits down across from him, and begins assailing the long-standing new-hire orientation program, Traditions. Despite the history and emotions connected to the Traditions program, Van pushes for a revision.
>
> "We need to revamp our Traditions program! We bring these kids into the university orientation for a full day of orientation and immediately start telling them about Disney history, traditions, and values and why this is such a great place to work. These are all great things, but at that time of the morning, do you know what these kids are really interested in learning about? They want to know where they will work, their schedule, what their costumes will look like, and how much they will be getting paid! Once they learn about the things that are important to them, they will be more receptive to listening to the things that are important

to us. We need to reverse the order of events and let these kids learn about some of these basic things that they are worried about."[13]

Darrell Metzger, the manager on the receiving end of Van's enthusiastic and unambiguous rant, says, "I worked with Van in the late 1970s, when I managed the Disney University at Disneyland. Van and I had a meeting, and he unexpectedly sprung on me the idea of revamping our Traditions new-hire orientation program."

Although the Traditions orientation had been the cornerstone program at the university for a number of years, Van wanted to change it. He argued that if the orientation program agenda was changed and employees were given specific job information in the morning, they would be more engaged later in the day; they would be attentive when they were presented with the company history and values and the Disney philosophy of service. Darrell continues, "It was so simple; we just reversed the order."

This represents one of the key lessons Darrell and many Disney University leaders learned from Van. Walking the park kept him in touch with the front lines, and he didn't hesitate to act on the information he gathered; he was an innovator. "Even though Van was in his late sixties, it was amazing to me how he could connect with and understand employees who were many years younger than he," says Darrell. "The Traditions orientation program was his baby, but he wasn't afraid to change it to make it better and keep it relevant."

Van France, the Mentor

Jim, that young Matterhorn supervisor approached by Walt Disney about improving operator training programs, followed Walt's suggestion (who wouldn't?) and met with Van France to learn more about Walt's reference to "something called the University of Disneyland."

Jim Cora, one of the four founding Disney University members enlisted by Van, worked many years with him and says, "Van was very creative. His background in the aircraft industry during World

War II taught him how to get things done quickly—due to the urgency of the war—and he shared those skills with us. Van taught us how to get around problems. Van taught me to think outside the box: don't accept everything you hear." Jim used those skills throughout his 43 years with Disney, leading the company's international expansions with Tokyo Disney Resort and Disneyland Paris Resort and retiring as chairman of Disneyland International.

What about that new program Jim proposed for training the Matterhorn operators? It was implemented and then refined into what became a new standard of training for Disneyland. Word-of-mouth training evolved into a standardized approach using checklists and operating manuals.

Decades later, in preparation for the opening of Tokyo Disneyland, Disney's first international theme park, the role of standardized training was further strengthened. As vice president of Walt Disney Productions Japan, Jim ensured that manuals were developed for every division and every discipline. "We introduced the Disney University concept to the Tokyo Disneyland staff and assured that we started with it at Disneyland Paris. Eventually, with Dick Nunis's support, manuals were required for all Disney Parks and Resorts worldwide," says Jim.[14]

Dick Nunis, Van's original protégé, was president of the Outdoor Recreation Division and a Disney corporate board member. Jim Cora, chosen by Van as a charter member of the Disney University, became chairman of Disneyland International. Both had roots in the Disney University and as senior executives of the company were indefatigable in their promotion of training.

Be Willing to Change or
Be Willing to Perish:
The Birth of the Disney University

More Than a University in Name Only

- Van continually evaluated the relevancy of orientation and training programs.

- Walt Disney helped Van recruit "young kids who had enthusiasm and experience working in operations." They added a vital component: credibility.

Disney University:
Where Everyone Majors in "People"

- Disney University was originally promoted as a vehicle to develop "Disneyland specialists," emphasizing leadership and people and trade skills.

- Technical and interpersonal skills are built on a solid foundation: a thorough understanding of the history and traditions of Walt Disney and his company.

- The goal of the Disney University is crystal clear: everyone majors in "people."

Tradition and Innovation

- Van's suggestion to reverse the order of events in the Traditions orientation program is illustrative of why the Disney University has remained relevant for so many decades:
  - Connection to the front lines
  - Willingness to change and innovate

- Like Walt, Van always had one foot in the past and one foot in the future.

Applying Van's Four Circumstances

INNOVATE ● SUPPORT ● EDUCATE ● ENTERTAIN

Be Willing to Change or Be Willing to Perish

In your organization, can you identify the equivalent of Van's Four Circumstances that support "be willing to change or be willing to perish" and balancing tradition with innovation? Can those things be applied to ensure that training and employee development programs are credible?

Does your organization recognize future leaders the way Walt Disney discovered Jim, the Matterhorn supervisor who became one of the founding members of the Disney University?

More Than a "University" in Name Only

- How does your training organization remain relevant and credible?

- How could training processes, programs, and staff improve "substance"?

Disney University:
Where Everyone Majors in "People"

- How clear is the mission of the training function in your organization?

- To what extent are the history and traditions of your organization perpetuated and built upon? How are they kept alive? How could this be improved?

Tradition and Innovation

- Which traditions should be maintained in your organization?

- Which traditions are impeding progress and innovation?

- Who in your organization has the influence and desire to implement change?

Simplify the Complex

Dick Nunis came up with a program which, at the time, was a totally new concept for operations. The four elements of theme park operations were listed in order of their importance.[1]

—**Van France**

The phone call from Michael Eisner came from out of the blue:

"Frank and I aren't pleased with what we have seen these past few days at the Disney Store. We noticed that the guest service experience isn't at the levels expected of Disney. The cast isn't as friendly or engaging as they should be, so aside from the product line, there isn't anything differentiating the Disney Store from all of the other stores at the Galleria.

We'd like the Disney University team to come up with a program to fix this problem and bring guest service up to Disney standards."

Michael Eisner, CEO of The Walt Disney Company, and Frank Wells, COO, weren't happy. The Disney Store, the company's first foray into a stand-alone retail environment, had a serious flaw. The first Disney Store, in the Glendale Galleria in California, was a short five-mile drive from The Walt Disney Company headquarters. Taking full advantage of the close proximity, Michael and Frank visited the store several times during the grand opening and the ensuing days of excitement.

For some, the excitement of the grand opening might have obscured the problems, but Michael and Frank noticed them. The flagship Disney Store, fresh out of the blocks in 1987, already needed upgrading; guest service wasn't even close to the Disney standards of excellence.

The Disney Store, not the Disney University, had created its own training program for its cast members, and it wasn't working. Seeking a solution, Michael Eisner called the Disney University.[2]

Bob De Nayer, whose 34-year Disney career took him from working as an hourly cast member in merchandise on Main Street at Disneyland to director of human relations at the corporate offices at Disney Studio, says, "Michael Eisner contacted my manager with the directive to get the guest experience at the Disney Store up to Disney standards." Saying that the training team at the Disney University went into emergency mode would be a vast understatement. The call from Michael came in on Friday afternoon. By the following Monday, they were ready with a completely revised orientation.[3]

Disney Guest Service:
Simplify the Complex With SCSE

Immediately after the call, the Disney University training staff embarked on a lightning-fast series of activities to create a brand-new orientation program. Despite the enormous pressure felt by all, nobody panicked. Relying on their years of theme park experience, each knew the path to success for the Disney Store and its cast members: the design of the new orientation program, *The Disney Shopping Experience*, had to simplify the complex. Cast members needed basic, sustainable, and memorable operations standards.

Confident that the Disneyland guest service and park operations strategy promoted by Van France and Dick Nunis would work equally well at the Disney Store, the training team simply followed its time-tested recipe plus the fundamentals extolled by Walt Disney. In a handbook for Disneyland hosts and hostesses, Walt writes,

> *What you do here and how you act is very important to our entire organization. [We have a] worldwide reputation for family entertainment. Here at Disneyland, we meet our world public on a person-to-person basis for the first time. Your every action (and mine also) is a direct reflection of our entire organization. So, it is vitally important to all of us to thoroughly understand our responsibilities, particularly our responsibility for guest relations and safety.*[4]

A theme park is like a giant factory. With literally millions of moving pieces and heavy equipment, it is a complex and potentially dangerous environment. In addition to the machinery, there is the cast; thousands of employees, both on-stage and backstage, taking care of the show. Into this environment of machinery and employees (the "factory") enters the guest. Guests come in all shapes, sizes, and ages. Some take their time and stroll about, whereas others never seem to slow down. Although diverse in age, ethnicity, and experience, most guests have one thing in common: they are in vacation mode. Enthralled with the environment, the costumes, and the attractions, many guests have no idea they have entered such a complex and potentially dangerous environment.

Providing The Happiest Place on Earth means that cast members must manage a delicate balance of priorities; without clarity, the task becomes overwhelming. Van France and Dick Nunis recognized the challenge. In response, they simplified this inherently complex environment by providing every cast member with crystal-clear marching orders during his or her Disney University orientation.

Dick's and Van's recipe for creating the magical environment at Disneyland involved boiling down park operations into four priorities that represent the values driving every decision:

1. **Safety.** This is the most important priority for guests and cast members. Cast members often must protect guests from themselves. Guests in vacation mode can become distracted by the colors, sounds, and activity. They aren't necessarily taking care of their own safety. The guest crossing Main Street may be completely unaware of the massive Percheron draft horse looming directly behind, pulling the trolley. Guests distracted by the beautiful architecture may walk straight into lampposts and walls. Every operations and design decision must first address safety.

2. **Courtesy.** The second most important priority after safety is courtesy. Cast members know the value of the smiles on their faces and in their voices and the importance of engaging guests. Directing a guest with an open hand and a smile is far more effective than pointing with one finger and scowling. A lack of cast member courtesy will poison the safest and most interesting environment.

3. **Show.** Once safety and courtesy are assured, attention turns to show. Well-maintained attractions and facilities populated by well-groomed cast members ensure good show, a condition Walt Disney passionately promoted. The antithesis is the Disney taboo: bad show.

4. **Capacity/efficiency.** This last priority refers to the number of guests enjoying the attractions, restaurants, and retail shops. This is the "hard numbers" portion of a business. By placing numbers last, the SCSE (safety, courtesy, show, and efficiency) model makes a clear, somewhat paradoxical statement; accom-

plishing the first three priorities ensures that this fourth one is sustainable in the form of happy and loyal cast members and guests.[5]

Each priority in this SCSE model is indispensable, and its position nonnegotiable. Although efficiency occupies the lowest rung on the priority ladder, it is by no means ignored. In fact, Disney Parks and Resorts invests heavily to ensure that the maximum number of guests can enjoy the facilities.

Yet the clarity of the SCSE model ensures that safety, courtesy, and show aren't sacrificed to attain more efficiency (more guests and higher profit). Efficiency initiatives must pass through the filter of the top three priorities.

The Disney Shopping Experience

Using the SCSE priorities as a guide, the Disney University trainers got to work on the training modules for the revamped Disney Store orientation program.

They first designed a strategy to assess the quality of customer service at the Disney Store. The needs assessment involved Disney University staff posing as customers ("secret shoppers") visiting the Disney Store, paying particular attention to cast members' interaction with customers. They would then compare their Disney Store experience with the levels of service they received as secret shoppers at other stores in the same shopping mall.

Armed with information about the state of the Disney Store and its competitors in the mall, the Disney University staff developed *The Disney Shopping Experience*, replete with SCSE-inspired clarity and simplicity.[6]

"Our goal was to instill a whole new level of enthusiasm and quality service with the staff of Disney Stores," says Bob. "I kept thinking about the lessons I learned so many years earlier from Van France. Van always reinforced the importance of keeping the message informative yet basic enough to be remembered and most of all—have fun!" Reinforcing this thought, Bob adds, "Van taught us that the more complicated the message, the more difficult to bring to life and maintain. So we set out to create a program that would be impactful, memorable, and, most of all, help differentiate Disney Stores from everyone else."

Within days of the phone call from Michael Eisner, Disney Store cast members found themselves participating in a completely revamped "Van France–style" training program. It meant closing the store for the day. Using the Disney Store as the classroom, the Disney University staff wasted no time getting cast members' full attention and participation. They kicked off the day by sending all cast members into the mall as secret shoppers to assess competitors' customer service.

Bob explains: "We gave each cast member a checklist of things to look for and questions to ask at the other stores during their secret-shopper experience:

- Were they and other customers greeted upon entering the store?

- Was the store clean?

- Were all the employees wearing clean clothes? If there was a "uniform," did all the employees wear it?

- Did employees engage them and other customers or just chat among themselves?

- Were employees visible and available for questions or too busy (folding clothes, restocking shelves)?

- Could employees answer questions about product sizing, store hours, and refund policies?

- Did employees lead customers to merchandise or merely point at the location?

* If employees didn't know the answer to a customer's question, did they seek the answer from a colleague?"

For the majority of cast members, the answer to each of these checklist questions was a resounding "no."[7]

This mini field trip opened cast members' eyes to the many "aha moments" for improving guest service at the Disney Store. Reporting their findings, Disney Store cast members shared a number of bad first impressions gathered during their secret-shopping experience:

"The clerk was on a personal telephone call," said one. "I felt like I was interrupting."

"There were only two employees working. They were chatting with each other and completely ignored me," said another.

"In our case, the person ringing us up at the register never looked at us or smiled. He acted like a robot," offered two more. "We were treated like an inconvenience."

Another added in disgust, "It's as if I was invisible; no one ever acknowledged me." Emphasizing his frustration, he continued: "They have cool stuff, but I won't go back to that store again."

Most prominent was cast members' collective shock regarding employees' indifference to customers and curious lack of product knowledge. Their competitors in the mall weren't consistently providing good, much less outstanding, customer service.

Leveraging this learning opportunity, the Disney University training staff then divulged vital information to the cast members: their recent experience as secret shoppers at the Disney Store had been painfully similar. Their experience as "customers" at the Disney Store was equally devoid of service, mediocre at best:

- Cast members in the role of greeters didn't engage guests in conversation.

- In some cases, guests were never acknowledged.

- Eye contact, smiles, and friendly tones of voice disappeared as the store got crowded.

- Cast members, intent on processing sales, focused more on the cash register operation than on guest interactions.

The Disney University staff wasn't alone in its unflattering assessment of the shopping experience at the Disney Store; Michael Eisner and Frank Wells felt the same way. This honest feedback from the training staff, coupled with the cast members' field trip observations, gave them a unique view of the condition of guest service at their Disney Store.

Good Show, Bad Show: The Living Classroom

Throughout *The Disney Shopping Experience,* the Disney University training staff employed multiple opportunities to reinforce service priorities. Just as Sophie experienced in her Disney University orientation, the connection between incessant attention to detail and outstanding guest service was constantly reinforced.

Intent on following Van and Dick's model for simplicity, the training staff introduced to the cast the SCSE operations model and the concept of good show versus bad show.

For example, during one of the breaks the staff purposely rearranged the environment in the Disney Store, creating bad show. They threw used napkins on the ground, moved chairs out of place, and didn't refresh the coffee. They even tilted some of the pictures on the wall. Pulling boxes and product off stockroom shelves and then randomly spreading them around the backstage area completed the scene.

In essence, the training team re-created the same disheveled atmosphere the cast members observed in other stores during their secret-shopping exercise. Once everyone returned to the Disney Store after the break, the training staff encouraged trainees to assess the condition of the room. According to Bob, "It took a while, but after we pointed out some of the aspects of bad show, the trainees really grasped what we were doing. In no time at all, they quickly pointed out things in the store that had to be refreshed, cleaned, or simply straightened up."

On the flip side, after a later break, the training staff went to great lengths to reinforce the Disney style of providing good show, much like that provided to Sophie during her Disneyland orientation. Bob explains, "During another break, we would straighten things up; we made sure notepads and pens were aligned on the desks, refilled ice and water in pitchers, put chairs back in rows; we even put sugar and sweetener packets in the same order at the coffee station. It might seem a bit over the top, but we wanted to reinforce Walt's and Van's timeless message of 'keep the place clean, fresh, and presentable.'"[8]

During these debriefing discussions, the trainers constantly reinforced the SCSE priorities. During the discussion of bad show, Bob asked cast members, "What have we done to negatively affect safety, courtesy, show, and efficiency?"

Citing safety, several shouted: "The boxes on the floor in the stockroom are a trip hazard!" Another chimed in, "Even though it's backstage, it looks bad, so isn't that also bad show?"

In a reference to courtesy, one said, "When I asked you how long this training program would last, you kept looking at the attendance roster on your computer while responding. You didn't look at me."

Examples of bad show abounded. "The dolls from the display cases aren't sitting up, plus some are on the floor," said one cast member. "The garbage can behind the counter is overflowing with paper and is in plain sight of the guests," offered another.

Addressing his comment to the training staff, one of the cast members offered his assessment of efficiency: "I think I finally understand the efficiency priority. In your secret-shopper assessment of the Disney Store, you said some of us were 'too busy' handling sales at the register." Looking a bit puzzled, he continued: "I thought I was doing a good job of handling the long lines in the store by quickly processing each sale. But my efficiency got out of control. I focused more on swiping credit cards and making change than on engaging guests in friendly conversations; you also said I was scowling."

Joining the efficiency discussion, another trainee added: "I tried to help move the line along at the counter by helping bag customers' purchases." With an introspective expression he added, "I saw an elderly couple; they were waiting patiently to ask a question. I got caught up bagging, and when I next looked up, they were leaving the store."

Cast members started to see the connection; safety, courtesy, and show couldn't be sacrificed by chasing after efficiency. Van and Dick's SCSE model of operational excellence, a proven success at Disney theme parks and resorts, resonated with the Disney Store trainees.

The interconnected nature of the SCSE priority model seemed to be making sense to the trainees when one shared a positive story. During her earlier secret-shopping experience at one of the other stores in the mall, the SCSE model came to life.

"I really enjoyed my experience at the coffee shop today," she said. "When I walked into the store, I saw an employee wiping up a coffee spill on the floor. That is an example of taking care of safety and show in one activity." Continuing, she said, "When I approached the counter, it was really crowded, but one of the employees immediately looked up, established eye contact, smiled, and said to me 'I'll be right with you.' That was a perfect demonstration of courtesy." Concluding her story, she said, "The menu board was easy to read and understand, which helped me quickly make my choice and kept the line moving, improving efficiency. Combined, each component created an environment of good show."

As the other trainees nodded their heads in agreement, the message was clear: the SCSE priority model, so effective at Disney theme parks and resorts, had a place in the retail environment.

Disney Characters to the Rescue

During their secret-shopper assessment of the Disney Store, Disney University staff observed cast members' lack of quality interaction with guests. Perfunctory greetings abounded:

"How are you today?"

"Can I help you find something?"

"Let me know if I can be of any help."

Definitely not the Disney Way.

These greetings created a first impression that was anything but unique. Disney Store cast members used the same tired greetings guests undoubtedly heard throughout the day at every other store in the mall.

Powerful, unique, and memorable first impressions such as those created by cast members at the Disney theme parks had to be addressed during *The Disney Shopping Experience*. How did the environment of Disney theme parks and the Disney Store differ? What enabled cast members at Disneyland to bridge those potentially awkward first few seconds of interaction with guests?

One of the answers was costumes. Costumes have tremendous inhibition-reducing qualities. Many theme park cast members enjoy the benefits of wearing fanciful costumes; they provide an instant connection with guests. After all, what cast member doesn't become a bit more extroverted after donning a Pirates of the Caribbean costume? The cast members at the Disney Store, although in a fanciful environment full of Disney characters, were dressed conservatively and acted accordingly. They needed a bridge.

For the Disney Stores, the solution came in the form of the very Disney character dolls surrounding them in the store. Those dolls, so beautifully displayed throughout the store, took on magical powers in the hands of the cast members.

Bob explains the transformative powers offered by the dolls: "Providing cast members a Disney character plush toy gave them license to interact with those guests walking by or already in the Disney Store." Simply holding up the plush toys attracted guests and helped cast members interact more freely. The toys, much like costumes at the theme parks, accomplished the same goal; by reducing cast members' inhibitions, they helped create powerful, unique, and memorable first impressions with guests. A cast member holding a Donald Duck doll has instantaneous guest relations power.

Adding to the challenge of the retail job is the guests' expectation surrounding any Disney experience. The Disney University team made sure the Disney Store cast members understood the value of creating that memorable first impression. In addition, cast members had to be prepared to answer questions seemingly unrelated to the Disney Store:

- What are the operating hours at Disney parks and resorts?

- What is the name of the upcoming Disney animated feature film?

- How much are theme park admission tickets?

- Where are the restrooms in the mall?

- What time does the mall close?

- Do they have a list of other stores in the mall?

From Pot of Soup to Bouillon Cube

The image of shrinking the massive and complex operations at Disneyland—the pot of soup—into the smaller, manageable bouillon cube via the SCSE priority model is powerful.

Simplifying the complex and clarifying priorities, the key lessons Van shared with legions of future Disneyland executives remain among the most important. Many who worked with Van are quick to offer testimonials reinforcing his lessons:

> "Van had an uncanny ability to articulate the complex."[9]

> "Van's secret was to keep things simple. The Disney service style is not complicated, and Van and Dick reinforced that idea. Both of them were straightforward with their message: do it right, nothing too flowery, nothing too sophisticated."[10, 11, 12]

> "Van made things so simple. For example, the concept of safety, courtesy, show, efficiency; this is easy to remember. In fact, the simplicity of it all still amazes me."[13]

Creating simplicity from complexity, the Disney University team successfully transferred the SCSE theme park operating principle to a retail environment. Following Van's timeless Four Circumstances, *The Disney Shopping Experience* helped perpetuate Walt's and Van's dream. The Disney Store is a unique environment, a friendly environment, a *Disney* environment.

Simplify the Complex

Good Show, Bad Show: The Living Classroom

- *The Disney Shopping Experience* remained true to one of Van's fundamental program designs; combining a succinct message with trainee interaction ensured that it was memorable and useful.

- Involving Disney Store cast members in secret-shopper assessments of competitors transformed them from passive trainees into active agents of change.

- Disney University staff transformed the Disney Store (their training room) into a living example of good show, bad show by purposely creating a disheveled environment.

Disney Characters to the Rescue

- Cast members, in their role as greeters, needed help. Their tired and overused phrases and strategies sabotaged efforts to create memorable first impressions.

- Disney plush toys sold in the store served double duty as icebreakers with guests. A cast member holding a Mickey Mouse doll has instant guest relations power.

Clear Priorities Are a Priority

- Safety, courtesy, show, and efficiency (SCSE) drive every decision at Disney theme parks and resorts.

- The brevity and simplicity of SCSE ensure retention and adherence; all Disney cast members know these priorities.

Applying Van's Four Circumstances

INNOVATE ● **SUPPORT** ● **EDUCATE** ● **ENTERTAIN**

Simplifying the Complex

How are complex operations and processes communicated in your organization? Are priorities succinct and memorable? How are Van's Four Circumstances used to convey complex and vital procedures and priorities?

It's All About the Basics

- How do you help employees understand standard operating procedures and priorities?

- Are employees actively involved as change agents, or do they wait for direction?

- Are policies followed? For example, are uniforms and safety gear consistently worn? If not, why?

Great Trainers Transfer Knowledge

- How does your training staff leverage experience from one division to another?

- What is your equivalent of using a plush toy Mickey Mouse doll to encourage interaction with customers, clients, or patients?

From Pot of Soup to Bouillon Cube

- What is your equivalent of SCSE?

- Can your employee manual be simplified? Shortened?

- What are your priorities? Can you summarize your standard operating procedures and priorities, regardless of complexity, with memorable phrases or acronyms?

The Honeymoon Will End

Cinderella Castle and Culture Change

As anyone who has been married knows, there is a difference between the moonlight and roses of courtship and the bills and responsibilities of marriage.[1]

—Van France

The Disney University staff looked around the room and knew that this was the perfect setting for the upcoming meetings with the division leaders. The room had no windows, nor was it painted. In fact, it was just an empty space left over from construction, no more glamorous than an unfinished attic. The meeting attendees would ascend to this location, high above the Magic Kingdom, via a small construction elevator or a steep, narrow staircase. The difficulty accessing the room made it all the more symbolic.

This would be an ideal backdrop for the sobering message soon to be shared: employee morale was spiraling out of control. The staff of the Disney University and the division leaders had to develop a plan to control the looming crisis.

The barometer of employee morale, the turnover rate, was hovering near 83 percent; employees were leaving the company in such high numbers that the recruiting and training teams could barely fill the gaps. They had long passed the service industry average of 55 percent. Also, those who remained were far from content. According to those closest to the issue, "Our house was on fire, and we needed to do something about it. Something had to change."[2]

The room, in the tower of Cinderella Castle, the symbol of The Happiest Place on Earth, would be a fine location for the meetings to come.[3]

The year 1973 ushered in a new era of growth for the Disney University. The fanfare and excitement accompanying the 1971 grand opening of the Magic Kingdom at Walt Disney World in Florida only 20 months earlier had disappeared. The first year of operations saw nearly 11 million guests pour through the park, leaving exhausted the thousands of cast members who had been carefully recruited and trained to get the park running and attend to the guests' every need. A softening economy and a reduction in the size of the workforce further added to the stress.

The 27,400 acres that constituted Walt Disney World made it almost 150 times the size of Disneyland in California.[4] At 43 square miles, it was a city unto itself, roughly equal in size to San Francisco and twice as big as Manhattan Island.

The Disney team had never managed an operation of that scale or complexity. Walt Disney World, complete with its hotels, resorts, golf courses, campgrounds, telephone company, utilities company, travel company, and Lake Buena Vista, was a far cry from the familiar confines of Disneyland.

At that time, the Magic Kingdom at Walt Disney World was the largest nongovernmental hiring and construction project in the United States. As construction drew to a close, staffing activities hit a mind-boggling pace. On opening day, there were more than 5,500 cast members. With only one of every eight applicants hired, the casting office screened well over 44,000 aspiring employees. By 1973, the original team of 5,500 cast members had ballooned to almost 10,000.

The size and scope of Walt Disney World were unprecedented. It faced an equally immense employee relations crisis.

The Walt Disney World Crisis

Anyone who has ever been involved in a grand opening knows the feeling. The energy accompanying the preopening, followed by the eventual letdown afterward, can be a daunting emotional roller coaster.

The crucible of preopening activities creates an intensity that is impossible to duplicate. The pressure-filled days, months, or years preceding a grand opening, replete with wild swings of creativity and anxiety, provide unparalleled growth opportunities. In contrast, the period that follows can be a bog of sameness; daily operations are rarely as invigorating or sexy as a grand opening.

At Walt Disney World, a number of issues were adding to the postopening blues:

- Roy Disney, who took over as the company's inspirational leader after Walt Disney's death in 1966, passed away in December 1971, barely two months after the opening of Walt Disney World. Roy, who assumed Walt's role of shepherding the development of Walt Disney World, was gone. His enthusiasm and focus motivated all the cast members to push through the challenges to complete Walt's Florida dream. The company lost its vital inspirational leaders in a relatively short span of time.

- Cast members were exhausted. There wasn't an operational road map for opening Walt Disney World. Since everything was so new, cast members learned as they created; systems and procedures were developed as the resort took shape. Three years of intense pressure, anticipation, and problem solving had taken their toll.

- Opportunities for career advancement slowed down. As the number and variety of job openings began to wane, many good cast members looked for career growth outside the company.

- Much more than a single theme park, Walt Disney World was a complex environment that involved many professions. Unlike Disneyland's early years, there wasn't a midwinter slowdown during which cast members could refurbish the property and take a well-deserved break. Walt Disney World, with the hotels, golf courses, campgrounds, and resorts, was a 24-hour-per-day, 365-days-of-the-year operation. The word *downtime* wasn't in the vocabulary. This was a different company.[5]

- Finally, the singular goal of opening Walt Disney World, a tremendous source of motivation in and of itself, was gone. What else was there to look forward to? The inspiration and motivation provided by the clarity of a major goal would be hard to duplicate.

The problems didn't occur overnight. As explained by one executive, "The three-year span of intense effort to build, staff, and then run Walt Disney World finally caught up to us. It wasn't like going to the doctor and suddenly finding out we had an incurable disease. It was more like we had slowly put on an extra thousand pounds and our health was now in jeopardy. Getting to the unhealthy state had taken several years, so regaining organizational health would involve much more than waving a magic wand." Recovery certainly wouldn't occur overnight.

The slump experienced by so many cast members at Walt Disney World is a challenge not uncommon in many companies after they have attained substantial goals. Employees and managers experience burnout.

Jack Lindquist, who was hired by Walt Disney just after Disneyland opened, was Disneyland's first advertising manager and was familiar with the pattern. Eventually rising to executive vice president of creative marketing concepts for Walt Disney Attractions and then president of Disneyland, Jack experienced multiple grand openings during his career, and he knows the toll a grand opening can exert on a team. Starting with Walt Disney World in Florida and then moving on to Tokyo Disneyland in Japan and Disneyland Paris in France, Jack relates his experiences: "Every grand opening team is the first wave, breaking new ground. I remember all of them. It's hell to go through, but in retrospect, we wouldn't miss it for the world."[6]

Sustaining the intense levels of preopening enthusiasm, effort, and momentum is not a reasonable goal for any organization. However, preventing a post accomplishment toxic work environment or a mass exodus of employees driven out by crashing morale is a goal that is both attainable and worth pursuing.

Cinderella Castle and Culture Change

The idea of using the room in the tower of Cinderella Castle as a meeting location belongs to Dick Nunis.[7] Dick knew that the castle, as the symbol of the company, would make a powerful statement about the importance of the meetings and the effort required of everyone.

Equally important would be the support and enthusiasm of those attending the meetings. When the director of the Disney University first met with Dick to outline a strategic plan, they agreed that the Disney University by itself couldn't drive organizational change without the support of those in operations. Every division had to collaborate.

As their meeting drew to a close, Dick picked up the telephone and personally called the vice presidents of every division, enlisting their support of the initiative to drive down turnover. He asked all of them to participate in the upcoming series of meetings in which they would help design a recovery strategy.

Dick didn't order the vice presidents to participate. They were well aware of the looming crisis and were completely behind the goal of reviving the spirit of Walt Disney World. The vice presidents, as well as their directors and managers, embraced the task as their personal responsibility. There was no need to cajole or convince them.

The Castle Meetings

The weekly meetings in Cinderella Castle set the stage for an eventual miraculous turnaround. Using a narrow set of stairs or the small elevator once used by construction crews, the director of the Disney University and the division vice presidents ascended the tower to reach the meeting room. Once there, they were greeted by stark surroundings most had never before seen: simple chairs surrounding a small table in a cramped and decidedly less than tidy atmosphere.

The setting alone underscored the importance of their upcoming task: to solve the employee morale and turnover crisis. As one attendee of those meetings stated, "The backstage room in the tower of Cinderella Castle helped set the tone and served as a way to further connect our leadership team to the front line, the park."

The first set of meetings involved just the division vice presidents. Eventually, the castle meetings evolved into sessions attended by their subordinates, the division directors. Within the first month, the directors and the Disney University team had created a plan for reducing employee turnover at Walt Disney World. It was far-reaching and demanded growth from everyone who participated:

- The Disney University, playing a central role in the turnaround initiative, developed into a sophisticated vehicle for employee development, communication, and care. Its traditional role of providing employee orientation programs, handbooks, and newsletters soon included activities supporting leadership and organizational development.

- A full-time human resources manager was added to each division. Those managers reported to both their division directors and the director of the Disney University, further strengthening collaboration between operations and those in the Disney University.

- Information from annual employee opinion polls and turnover data drove decisions.

- The Disney University collaborated with every division to create a human resources plan that was based on the data gathered from employees.

Data Drive Change

The divisional human resources managers, taking over from the divisional vice presidents and directors, began meeting regularly with the staff of the Disney University. Using the castle meeting room, they met for many months, setting employee training and development goals, devising objectives, and analyzing turnover numbers.

Extensive use of employee opinion polls provided crucial information to the executive team. Poring over the data revealed the following:

- Those in operations were experts at keeping the show up and running.

- The human resources staff expertly handled labor relations, compensation, employment, and new hires.

- Cast members, the company's most important asset, felt lost in the shuffle.

Several executives who were familiar with the issues learned, in the words of one of them, "We had put a lot of effort into attending to the needs of our external customers, but now we needed to ramp up our *internal* customer service."[8]

The Centralized and Decentralized Approach

The meetings in Cinderella Castle, which were ultimately moved to a meeting room in the Disney University, led to a revised employee development strategy, the centralized and decentralized approach: *centralized,* meaning those activities controlled by the Disney University, and *decentralized,* referring to activities under the control of the divisions.

Thor Degelmann's description clarifies the roles: "At the center is the Disney University. It is the keeper of the key, the company's conscience regarding the Disney brand; it is responsible for setting the 'big picture' to ensure a consistent delivery of the product. The new-hire orientation ensures everyone coming on board knows the culture of the company. The *decentralized* portion of the training strategy is the responsibility of each operating division. Task-specific training such as cash-handling, food safety, and daily operations details are the responsibility of the operating divisions."[9]

This shared approach reinforces the importance of everyone having accountability for and ownership of cast member development. It also recognizes the uniqueness of every division and allows for some customization of training and communication.

The staff of the Disney University built on Van France's vision of a university "that was ahead of the times, leading people into exciting adventures." The employee opinion polls also contributed to three expansion initiatives involving training and development, cast activities, and cast communications.

Initiative 1: Enhanced Training and Development

The training function was vastly expanded to include far more than new-hire orientation. Programs and curricula were created to help the professional development of employees at all levels:

- Hourly cast members were able to participate in cast development programs.

- Supervisors and managers could choose from a variety of management development courses.

Even the new-hire orientation process was further developed to ensure that every cast member received engaging, consistent, and relevant training. A four-day onboarding process was developed that employed the centralized and decentralized approach; the Disney University and each operations division filled vital roles. The staff of the Disney University conducted the detailed company orientation on the first day, during which all cast members were welcomed in the same way and in which all participated.

The ensuing three days of training were conducted in the operations divisions. Food and beverage, finance, security, merchandise, and every other division created its own programs, with a curriculum ranging from a general introduction to the division to job-specific training. Cast members from each division who were certified by the Disney University as "qualified division trainers" provided the training. Even when not directly conducting training, the Disney University ensured training consistency and quality.

Initiative 2: Expanded Cast Activities

The meetings in Cinderella Castle also reinforced the need to expand support and recreational and social opportunities for cast members. Cast members, through the opinion poll, revealed needs that had never before been addressed; they felt the company could provide more assistance in their roles as employees, as parents, and as social beings in an increasingly complex and growing environment. Van France's original Disneyland Recreation Club, now known as Cast Activities, could play an even more significant role at Walt Disney World. The large number of cast members created challenges never before faced at Disneyland, yet this large employee population was balanced by the vast expanse of property available at Walt Disney World. Opportunities for recreational and support activities abounded:

- A 60-acre area at Little Lake Bryan was transformed into a recreation area specifically for cast members (now smaller and known as Mickey's Retreat). This unique environment enabled the company to provide not only the requisite fields for sporting events and picnic grounds but also a lake for fishing and boating.

- A day care center for cast members' children was created.

- Because of soaring gasoline prices in the Orlando area, a gas station was built that offered subsidized prices.

Initiative 3: Unique Cast Communications

The Disney University staff and division human resources managers designed creative ways to connect with cast members:

- Whimsical billboards strategically placed on the property greeted cast members with important and timely messages, including holiday-specific greetings.

- Remodeled and upgraded break areas, cafeterias, and wardrobe dressing rooms conveyed to the cast members the importance of their comfort.

- Tunnels running under the Magic Kingdom, the passageways cast members use to get from break rooms and dressing rooms to work, weren't exempt from the freshening up. As one executive stated, "We didn't want cast members to feel like rats in a tunnel." Those concrete tunnels, once dull and drab, were transformed into bright and inviting spaces.

- Motivational and birthday messages created in each division and added to paycheck envelopes lent a more personal touch.

- Informational videos broadcast over a closed-circuit system and updated weekly appeared on television monitors in the break rooms.

- The Walt Disney World newsletter, *Eyes and Ears of Walt Disney World*, well liked and widely read by cast members, remained a valuable tool by which to share information.

Unprecedented Results

By 1975, two years after the commencement of the meetings in Cinderella Castle, the turnover rate at Walt Disney World had dropped from a dismally high 83 percent to 28 percent, a 66 percent relative reduction in turnover. The numbers, viewed from the opposite perspective of employee retention, reveal the impressive results. The initial anemic 17 percent employee retention rate grew to 72 percent, a stunning fourfold increase.

In isolation, none of the activities, meetings, or initiatives could have led to such a mind-boggling drop in turnover. The most important factor in this organizational evolution was the cumulative effect.

Dick Nunis, the man first hired and trained by Van France, was consistently and directly involved in the success of the Disney University and the cast members. By personally calling the vice presidents of each division to request their support, Dick set the stage for leadership involvement. As president of the Outdoor Recreation Division, he felt strongly that it was his job and shouldn't be delegated or relinquished. His decision to conduct weekly meetings in Cinderella Castle, one of the most recognized symbols of the company, further underscored the gravity of the crisis.

The Disney University, as the vehicle for employee development, communication, and care, didn't have to act alone. The collaboration between the Disney University and each operations division reflects the enthusiasm with which the leadership of every division at Walt Disney World attacked this crisis.

The honeymoon was over, but the marriage would thrive.

The Honeymoon Will End:
Cinderella Castle and Culture Change

The Honeymoon Will End

- The type of morale slump experienced after the opening of Walt Disney World is a challenge for many companies; some level of employee and manager burnout is normal.

- Preopening levels of intensity, enthusiasm, effort, and momentum waned.

- Preventing a postevent environment of crashing morale is a reasonable goal that is worth pursuing.

- Even a team of all-stars must communicate and collaborate.

Symbols Are More Powerful
Than Words

- Dick Nunis's personal phone calls to each divisional vice president carried immense weight. He didn't delegate the task.

- Convening meetings in Cinderella Castle sent an unmistakable message of urgency to the leadership team.

- Inviting employees to critique the company via opinion polls and then acting on the information shared creates an environment of trust.

Synergy and Collaboration
Are Unstoppable Forces

- The Cinderella Castle meetings helped deepen trust, respect, and communication between the staff of the Disney University and the operations staff.

- Data and metrics formed the basis for development plans. The employee opinion polls, combined with the turnover rates, provided ample information.

- The centralized and decentralized approach led to more effective cast member training and communication.

- Cast member development and morale belonged to every division; the Disney University didn't act alone.

Applying Van's Four Circumstances

INNOVATE ● **SUPPORT** ● **EDUCATE** ● **ENTERTAIN**

Crisis Management and Culture Change

How are crisis management and culture change handled in your organization? How are Van's Four Circumstances used to improve employee morale?

The Honeymoon Will End

- In your organization, what is the equivalent of a honeymoon coming to an end? How is this change being addressed?

- Are executives fully engaged in the resolution process? Who is involved and with what frequency?

- How could this turnaround strategy be improved?

- If this is not being done, what is the excuse for inactivity?

Symbols Are More Powerful Than Words

- What symbols represent the culture of your organization (people, products, structures, logos)?

- How could these symbols be used to help reinforce organizational culture and resolve crises? Are they being used now? How? If not, why?

- How do you communicate important messages?

Synergy and Collaboration
Are Unstoppable Forces

- In your organization, what is the equivalent of Cinderella Castle meetings, Dick Nunis telephone calls, and a centralized, decentralized employee development strategy?

- Are openness, honesty, and collaboration encouraged? If not, why? What needs to be done?

- Do you conduct employee opinion polls? If not, why? If so, do you act on the data?

Keep Plussing the Show

No Room for Excuses

We have to keep plussing our show. If we ever lose them [the guests], it will take us ten years to get them back.[1]

—**Walt Disney**

Van France is frustrated by the "victim mentality" he sees starting to creep into the management team at Disneyland. It is 1980, and three converging forces are taking their toll:

- The worldwide recession and the resultant drop in guest visits to Disneyland are creating tremendous pressure for the managers; they and their cast members must do more with less.

- The development of EPCOT in Florida, opening in just two years, is stretching already thin corporate resources, both financial and human.

- Tokyo Disneyland, the company's first international theme park, is scheduled to open in three years and is further depleting limited resources.

All three forces are creating unprecedented challenges for the management team. Also, the economic and business realities aside, the lack of attention directed to Disneyland doesn't sit well with the management team at the park. Sharing the stage is a new concept for them; Disneyland is no longer the only star. Van is concerned that the world-famous Disneyland guest service will suffer as a result. He attacks the problem head on; the time is right for an attitude adjustment.

Determined to reignite the can-do culture at Disneyland, Van prepares for the management a team refresher course called *Gentlemen, This Is a Guest!* Using a decidedly low-budget and bare-boned approach, Van is out to make the point that there is room for improving customer service at Disneyland and the complaining should stop. Neither the weak economy nor the corporate attention paid to Florida and Japan will get in his way. Never one to back down, Van argues, "It is truly head-in-a-hole thinking not to face up to the serious effects that inflation and recession will eventually have on our attendance."[2, 3] Van is convinced that the time is right for "plussing the show."

Passages from the course materials exemplify Van's approach:

- "If we don't provide what the Guest pays for, you and I are all going to be out on our individual [backsides], looking for some other way to make a living."[4]

- "There is not one darned thing that you or I can do about the recession, depression, bankruptcies, unemployment or interest rates. But there *are* things that you or I *can do* about improving the friendliness, fun, showmanship and general happiness of the guests who pay us. We are in the unique position where each of us can do something to protect our own jobs and careers by improving the show. With all due respect to the excitement in Florida and Japan, we are here where it all started. Our job is to work together to preserve this dream which made all other growth possible."[5]

The Disneyland managers are facing a paradox: how best to deal with the effects of an economic bust and boom occurring simultaneously. Through his *Gentlemen, This Is a Guest!* sessions, Van plans to reconnect the management team with the roots of excellence that have served Disneyland so well.

Boom or Bust and Everything in Between

The extremes of economic booms and busts will never vanish. Both create considerable angst among leaders, and no one is immune. Leaders in government, business, religious institutions, nonprofits, and start-up organizations all face similar challenges.

Boom and bust extremes force leaders to consider ways to address the following challenges:

- Do more with less

- Keep employees engaged and motivated

- Reduce employee turnover

- Improve customer service

- Differentiate from the competition

Differentiation is the ultimate goal: how to stand out as the employer of choice, vendor of choice, service provider of choice—the *whatever* of choice.

Differentiating by doing more with less, keeping employees engaged and motivated, and improving customer service is now more of a constant than an aberration. The anxiety and stress that used to be felt only during the extremes of boom and bust is a daily reality for many.

The strongest leaders know the importance of differentiating during the time between the twin crises of boom and bust. Fortunately, there is a growing body of leaders who realize that product development alone (whether a service or an actual product) isn't sufficient. To differentiate, these leaders know they also must improve their employee training and development strategies.

In the hectic dash to evolve and differentiate from the competition through training, the links between organizational values, clear training goals, employee needs, and customer demands can weaken. Even organizations that usually are guided by the equivalent of the values embodied in Van's Four Circumstances—innovate, support, educate, and entertain—would do well to assess if and when they lose sight of their values: What drives them into a knee-jerk reaction mode?

The wild ride on the economic roller coaster quickly gets out of control when values are jettisoned and excuses start flying.

Boom, then bust.

Blame the Economy

Somewhere in the world, the following two scenarios are currently being played out. Both reflect a passive, victim mentality. Both undermine sustained employee and organizational development. Both open the door to competitors.

Scenario 1: Bust

"This weak economy is killing me. 'Do more with less' is the name of the game. My budgets are slashed, and I have no wiggle room."

The result?

- I don't have the budget, time, or people for training.

- Why train employees? They'll be gone pretty soon.

Scenario 2: Boom

"This booming economy is killing me. We're barely filling existing orders, plus I can't keep my good people. They jump ship as soon as someone else comes along waving a little extra money."

The result?

- I don't have the time or people for training.

- Why train employees? They'll be gone pretty soon.

Blaming the economy is a convenient excuse for not providing training.

It's Not the Economy: Some Organizations Aren't Ready for Training

Two organizations are at opposite ends of the economic spectrum: one is in a dying environment, and the other is in a thriving environment. Yet the economy aside, there are surprising similarities between the two in one area. The odds are good that neither organization has a history or culture of providing useful employee training that is supported by the top leaders.

Before these organizations commit to offering any sort of training, they should address the following questions:

- How effective have training programs been in the past?

- How did those training programs contribute to the bottom line?

- How did those training programs contribute to the emotional health of employees?

- Who was the biggest cheerleader for training: the training manager, the CEO, or the employees?

All too often, the answers to these four questions are "I don't know," "I don't know," "I don't know," and "The training manager."

If this is the case, developing and implementing training probably isn't a good idea for either organization. They aren't ready. Training would most likely prove counterproductive and harmful to the organizational health of both. Pulling people from their real jobs into poorly designed training is a waste of resources and time and will undermine morale.

It doesn't have to be this way. Also, don't blame the economy; that's the most convenient excuse for cutting training.

Keep Plussing the Show

Walt Disney's admonition to "keep plussing our show" is simply another way of saying "keep improving product and service." Among cast members there is a well-known story about Walt's commitment to constant improvement. It involves a disagreement Walt had with his Park Operating Committee (POC), the team charged with running Disneyland. Over the objections of the POC, Walt approved funding Disneyland's first Christmas parade, which evolved into a much-anticipated annual event. Walt based his argument on the need to keep "plussing" the show, to keep improving the product and service.

Through his *Gentlemen, This Is a Guest!* sessions, Van embarked on a similar mission to keep plussing the show. He identified a need to reignite the passion and can-do attitude among managers at Disneyland. Undeterred by the dual challenges of economic uncertainties and unprecedented growth, Van focused on plussing the basics. In fact, he even cited the famous Walt-versus-the-POC incident in his curriculum to reinforce the age-old message from the founder: "The best is never the best."[6]

Utilizing nothing more than a 15-page memo and a series of short, open forum–style meetings with Disneyland management, Van helped a discouraged team reconnect with its roots by emphasizing Disneyland's bottom line: a happy guest. He also reminded the managers of their role in the show by entreating them to do the following:

- *Think teamwork.* Thinking "we" is much more powerful than thinking "they," "them," "the young people," or "the unions." Blaming is a bottomless pit.

- *Think audience and guest.* Referring to guests merely as "attendance numbers" is dehumanizing. Guests are the audience, paying money to be entertained and find happiness. Guests aren't "units" or "per capita"; they are human beings.

- *Think happiness for others.* Guests come to Disneyland seeking happiness; it is their brief escape from daily frustrations. Walt Disney's dream of separating the frustrating outside world from the Disneyland world ensures guest happiness. Maintaining an environment of fantasy is our job.

- *Practice being friendly.* Smile and be friendly with each other. Saying good morning to each other backstage will transfer to friendliness on-stage.

- *Think quality and pride.* Both are essential in guest courtesy and showmanship, throughout our backstage activities as well as those on-stage.[7]

None of Van's admonitions are expensive. None require investments in fancy new cast member costumes or upgraded attractions.

Plussing the show is as much about attitude as it is about budget.

We Sell Pixie Dust!

Certainly, Van faced his share of tough questions and challenges. Especially during the economic and growth challenges mentioned above, a good number of cast members and managers would throw down the gauntlet and question the whole "happiness thing" by saying, "Don't give us that pixie dust." In those instances, Van rapidly was transformed into what Dick Nunis aptly called "an angry Donald Duck."[8] Van let employees know in no uncertain terms that pixie dust *was* the product and they needed to have pride in providing it to guests: "Selling pixie dust? You're damned right. That's what we do and I'm proud of it."[9]

Van knew when to be flexible and when to draw the line. There was no ambiguity in his approach. He wasn't a slick-talking corporate politician but a brutally honest cheerleader. Van's lesson of clarity and honesty in *Gentlemen, This Is a Guest!* is one of the many reasons for the enduring culture of happiness at all Disney theme parks and resorts. Everyone knows the real product, and it is much more than parades, rides, and costumed characters.

No Excuses

Keenly aware that "the word *training* has a nauseating effect on some people,"[10] Van didn't hesitate to challenge poorly designed or outdated training programs. He was the first person to change or eliminate a training event if he felt it wasn't getting results. He also knew that training alone wasn't the answer; training couldn't solve every problem.

Van was equally ardent in challenging excuses for not conducting training. Like Walt Disney, Van rejected the notion that economic malaise warrants abandoning efforts to plus the show. Bill Ross recalls a valuable lesson: "Van firmly believed in employment development activities and didn't let a slim budget get in the way. Money might be tight; creativity is free."[11] Even more direct is Van's message in a report titled *Disneyland: The Exciting New Era, 1980–2005:* "The budget has become the scapegoat for every possible negative action and rejection of any suggestion for improving things. It is the coward's way out of any problem."[12]

Training doesn't have to be a big-budget extravaganza or be limited to activities in a training room. Some of the best training in the world occurs during on-the-job-training (OJT) sessions conducted by mentors, not trainers. Mentoring, OJT, and role modeling can be much more useful and significantly less expensive than classroom training. Weekly staff meetings and five-minute preshift/postshift "huddles" provide tremendous training and learning opportunities.

Jim Cora sums up the training rationale he successfully used during his 43-year career at Disney:

> *Marketing is the time and money you spend to get people in the door. Training is the investment you make to get guests to come back and cast members to stay; it creates loyalty. If show was affected, I never cut corners to save money. I never canceled a training program if it helped our show.*

Plussing the show calls for a keen eye, the ability to focus on the root issues, and a refusal to accept mediocrity. Picture, for example, the bales of hay in Frontierland. Strategically placed as props to enhance the western feel, they are a vital component of the show. Now imagine weeds sprouting from those bales; that is bad show, a Disney taboo. Is this a "training situation" in which the groundskeepers need additional training on the proper trimming of weeds? Continuing with his description of plussing the show, Jim explains when training isn't the answer: "If weeds are growing out of the hay bales in Frontierland, then the bales should have been replaced long ago."[13]

Keep Plussing the Show:
No Room for Excuses

No Excuses, No Complaints

- The combined effects of building two new theme parks and getting through a soft economy put enormous strain on Disneyland managers to do more with less.

- Envious of the attention directed toward the newer parks, the Disneyland management team began exhibiting signs of indifference toward guests and cast members.

Boom or Bust: Both Can Kill Training Programs

- Both a booming economy and a dying economy create perfect excuses for eliminating training programs.

- Training programs are often the first thing to go when organizations are forced to do more with less.

- Walt Disney's admonition to "keep plussing our show" is simply another way of saying, "Keep improving the product and service."

Plus the Show

- Van's management refresher course *Gentlemen, This Is a Guest!* aligns perfectly with Walt's determination to constantly upgrade regardless of economic reality.

- Plussing the show is as much about attitude as it is about budget.

Applying Van's Four Circumstances

INNOVATE ● SUPPORT ● EDUCATE ● ENTERTAIN

Plussing the Show

How is plussing the show handled in your organization? How are Van's Four Circumstances used to differentiate your organization from the competition through improved customer service and management effectiveness?

Boom and Bust Extremes: What Are Your Issues?

How are you addressing each of the following five challenges?

- Doing more with less

- Keeping employees engaged and motivated

- Reducing employee turnover

- Improving customer service

- Differentiating from the competition

Some Organizations Aren't Ready for Training

- Has training harmed your organization (morale, productivity, bottom line)?

- What caused this, lack of training effectiveness or lack of leadership support?

- How can you prevent this from happening again?

- How creative is your organization at taking training out of the classroom?

Gentlemen, This Is a Guest!

- How can you reignite the flagging spirits of your team? Can you create a similarly effective low-budget program that helps plus your service or product?

Beyond Orientation

Executive Development:
From Silos to Synergy

Walt was very firm in stating that Disneyland—the dream—was the star. It was his way of controlling the people with their outsized egos who thought that they or their divisions, departments, or functions were responsible for our success.[1]

—**Van France**

Frank Wells, the COO of the Walt Disney Company, couldn't have been happier. The results of the executive seminar designed and implemented by the Disney University were just what he envisioned.

Frank places a telephone call to the manager of the Disney University at The Disney Studio and says, "Michael [Eisner] and I can already see the benefits of 'Disney Dimensions.' It has changed the dynamics between the operating units by building bridges across what had become silos. This program has enabled people to see the bigger picture."[2]

From Silos to Synergy

The seminar, called "Disney Dimensions," was in direct response to a problem at the Disney Studio: communication silos inadvertently created several years earlier by Frank Wells and Michael Eisner. Michael Eisner, chief executive officer and chairman of the board, and Frank Wells, chief operating officer, were brought on board in 1984 to turn around the corporation. Reeling after barely surviving several leveraged buyout attempts, the company had been in danger of being dismantled.

As part of the strategy to reinvigorate the Disney Studio—and the whole company—Michael and Frank were determined to foster a culture of creativity, innovation, and accountability. Several years after they joined the company, the new entrepreneurial culture they created was already reaping great rewards; the 1989 smash hit *The Little Mermaid* was a direct result. But there was also an unintended negative consequence.

According to Carol Davis-Fernald, who started as a trainer in the Disney University and rose to the position of vice president of human resources and employee Initiatives, "One of the unforeseen outcomes of the entrepreneurial culture Michael and Frank created was silos. People got so focused on their areas of responsibility that they didn't consider their impact on other divisions, departments, or business units. Executives kind of lost sight of the big picture, and we lost some opportunities for synergy."

Even All-Stars Must Communicate

One of those lost opportunities was associated with that very movie, *The Little Mermaid*. Carol continues: "*The Little Mermaid* was a blockbuster hit at the theaters, but we didn't fully leverage that success in consumer products; retail sales of *The Little Mermaid*–themed merchandise such as dolls and games didn't fare as well as they could have."

The problem was product volume and variety. In light of the unparalleled success of the movie, there was a lack of mermaid-themed merchandise in stores. The consumer products team hadn't been involved in developing merchandise until late in the game, and since the product development cycle—from initial ideas to products on store shelves—is long, there hadn't been time to catch up. The problem was due to the communication silos. The lack of timely communication and collaboration between business units had become a major problem.

Much as was the case in the situation with the Disney Stores project, Frank and Michael asked the Disney University team to help improve collaboration between the business units. Bob De Nayer, the Disney University training director who helped create the program with Carol Davis-Fernald, says, "We went back to the basics even though the participants in Disney Dimensions were at and above the vice president level."[3] The Disney University team created an experience for the executives that borrowed from Van's timeless model for any training program:

- Make it simple (not simplistic).

- Make it enjoyable.

- Design experiential activities that make it memorable.

Staying true to Van's approach, the Disney University team created a program that achieved Michael and Frank's goal of improving communication and creating more synergy between their teams of high-powered and accomplished executives.

Executive Development: A Disney Tradition

In addition to drawing on Van's legacy of highly interactive training programs, the Disney University team had another Disney training legacy from whom to borrow creative inspiration. Mike Vance, who had been hired by Walt Disney in the mid-1960s to create and lead executive-level training and development programs, designed the first educational seminars for senior staff.

According to Mike, "Walt posed an interesting challenge. He asked me to create programs that would encourage participants to reach out and try new approaches. But Walt also cautioned me to think things through carefully. He didn't want quickly thrown together, seat-of-the-pants events."[4]

Mike continues: "Walt was emphatic in his desire to 'see what people are thinking.'" Therefore, Mike created an interactive program for the executive teams that allowed participants and facilitators to more clearly see what each was thinking and doing. The program Mike developed took place over several months and involved taking senior executives on tours of every business unit to ensure that everyone on the team knew the role each person played. Armed with Walt's "seeing is believing" model, Mike infused the programs, originally called Disney Way I and Disney Way II, with highly interactive learning components; Mike's design ensured that learning occurred in multiple environments, using a combination of experiential and theoretical tools.

The infamous character experience during which executives get a chance to spend part of the day as one of the famous Disney costumed characters (think Tigger) is the epitome of engagement. What could be more impactful than donning a costume of sweaty fur, plopping on a huge helmet shaped like a tiger's head, and then wading into a mass of eager guests, all determined to get a photograph or autograph? Within moments, executives see the reality of the front lines. Mike leveraged Walt's technique of using engaging visuals, props, and storyboards when presenting ideas. Mike adds: "We created programs with the following in mind: If you could sit down and talk with Walt, what would you get?"

Disney Dimensions built on time-tested models for creating an engaging, memorable, and useful executive seminar. Twenty-five executives representing every business unit in the corporation participated in Disney Dimensions. These senior executives from parks and resorts, consumer products, imagineering, the studio, and eventually the Disney-owned ESPN and ABC also brought a varied mix of Disney experience. Some executives were new to the company, whereas others had been with Disney for a number of years. Each attendee, personally selected by Michael and Frank, knew the importance of and support behind Disney Dimensions.

Carol adds: "We had them for seven very full days, and we set out to give them the complete Disney experience. We gave them tours of our parks and resorts in California and Florida. We also had interactive sessions at the studio and Imagineering. We had them analyze case studies—we got them talking. Essentially, we exposed them to every business unit in the company and had them solving each other's problems."

The Little Mermaid Revisited

There was even a day during the week when the lost merchandising opportunities from *The Little Mermaid* were examined. Retailing specialists from consumer products were brought in to share research data with the executives. The missed opportunities with *The Little Mermaid* that had resulted from a lack of communication and a full understanding of the marketplace became crystal clear. "When the consumer products experts explained the 'play patterns' of little girls with mermaid dolls, patterns that had not been understood by scriptwriters and those who marketed the movie, every executive in the room reacted in the same way: 'Look at the opportunity we missed,'" says Carol. The importance of involving a more diverse team, even from the earliest levels of script development, became one of the many learning points garnered by those attending Disney Dimensions.

The tremendous increase in the volume of merchandise sales for subsequent films such as *Beauty and the Beast* and *The Lion King* provides testimony to the power of improved communication and the synergy that Disney Dimensions helped foster.

The Green Light Experience

The Disney University team kept Van's mantra of simple, enjoyable, and memorable alive with an exercise called the Green Light Experience. The exercise resonated particularly well with all the participants in that the words *green light* are deeply rooted in the film industry. It brought to life the challenges every participant in the Disney Dimensions program faced in his or her own division. Giving the green light to a project means giving the final approval. Since every participant was at or above the vice presidential level, each knew intimately the immense complexity and pressure that accompanies approving projects of such importance. Adding complexity to any go/no-go decision of this significance is the inevitable criticism of the final decision: it's impossible to please everyone.

According to Bob, "We wanted every participant in Disney Dimensions to really *connect* with each other, so we created a number of experiential exercises. Our goal was to keep the program relevant, not theoretical, and have fun while learning. Several of us on the team learned this from Van, and we were determined to employ his approach." The program design constantly reinforced vital goals with each participant:

- The benefits of utilizing the collective expertise residing in the company

- The value of increased communication and collaboration between business divisions

At the outset of the Green Light Experience, all the participants received two different movie scripts to assess and were told to decide which script they would green-light. Although their decision

wouldn't extend beyond the training room, the participants enthusiastically tackled the assignment.

A fact not divulged to the participants when they received the
scripts was that one script had already been green-lit by the Disney
Studio and would soon go into production.

The next day, during the debriefing phase of the exercise, the
executive in charge of film production at the Disney Studio first
asked the participants to disclose which script they had selected
and their rationale for doing so. After this debriefing discussion,
the participants learned about the actual production plans for the
script already green-lit by the Disney Studio. Furthermore, executives from marketing, distribution, legal affairs, and production
shared details about their roles in the green light process.

"This exercise was great in that it helped our executives understand how movie projects evolve and the vast number of variables
that influence which get the go-ahead, from the creative aspect to
the hard business numbers," says Carol. Senior executives participating as Disney Dimensions presenters and facilitators added vital
credibility and urgency. Carol adds, "When the chairman of Walt
Disney Studios, Dick Cook, sits down with the group to discuss the
business of making and distributing films, everyone listens." Dick,
who was instrumental in creating the highly successful *Pirates of
the Caribbean* film franchise and the purchase of Marvel Entertainment, had ample experience with the green light process.

Although Dick spent most of his 38-year career at the Disney Studio, he started at Disneyland as an attractions host at the
Monorail and the Disneyland Railroad. His Disneyland training experience greatly influenced his leadership approach at the Disney
Studios. Dick explains, "The first time I met Van France was in my
new-hire orientation. There was a new Disney University trainer
conducting the training, and he was having some difficulty. It was
his first day conducting orientation, and he was scared to death.
Throughout the day, Van helped this guy out. Van would step in and
coach him. It wasn't until the end of the session that we found out

who Van was. How unassuming and helpful! As I worked my way through the company, I often thought of Van; he wasn't too big to participate."[5]

Everyone Becomes an Imagineer

A similarly engaging exercise at Walt Disney Imagineering had the same executives brainstorming designs for a theme park attraction. Marty Sklar, the vice chairman of Walt Disney Imagineering, remembers, "We had the Walt Disney Imagineering staff lead these teams of executives in the creative and collaborative process of designing a new theme park attraction. We divided them into small groups of four each, assigned an imagineer to each team, and then gave them 90 minutes to complete the task."[6]

As each team proudly divulged its new attraction concepts, Marty and his imagineering team engaged them in discussions about their creative process: What drove their decision, and did they fully utilize the wisdom of everyone in the group?

The Green Light Experience and the Walt Disney Imagineering team exercises became the vehicles for participants to discuss company-specific issues in a risk-free environment. As simple as it might sound, this simple act of communicating helped improve trust and increased awareness of the collective wisdom residing in all the business units.

These exercises also reinforced the need for the executives to perpetuate the communication and synergy developed during their week at Disney Dimensions; the ongoing health of the company was on the line. A box-office blockbuster creates numerous opportunities for synergy between consumer products (videos, dolls, costumes, toys, electronic games, etc.) and the attractions and parades featured at Disney Parks and Resorts. In addition, hit movies can lead to big-budget musicals and entire areas ("lands") in theme parks.

The reverse is also true. A wildly successful attraction at the theme parks can serve as a catalyst for live-action movies. Exemplifying this synergy is the perennially popular Pirates of the Caribbean attraction, which opened at Disneyland in 1967. Decades after its debut, this attraction led to the hugely successful series of *Pirates of the Caribbean* feature films and a new stream of pirate-themed consumer products.

Executives Walk the Park

The communication silos at the Disney Studio bore a strong resemblance to the gap between the maintenance and park operations staffs Van discovered many years earlier during one of the many times he walked the park. Similar to the challenges Van and his original training faced, the Disney University team at the studio knew they had to reduce the barriers between operating units to improve communication and ultimately improve business results. They used every opportunity to showcase the role each business unit played in the overall Disney show.

In addition to the activities at the Disney Studio and Walt Disney Imagineering, Disney Dimensions participants experienced the unique cultures of ESPN and Disney Parks and Resorts. During the entire week, the Disney University team went to great lengths to reinforce the fundamental Disney Parks and Resorts strategy of providing outstanding customer service—good show—to their guests, the Disney Dimensions trainees. For example, according to Bob, "We took care of everything for the attendees so that they could focus on the program. Plus we used every possible opportunity to drive home the importance of customer service, teamwork, and the Disney Way." Included in Disney Dimensions were tours of the parks and resorts in California and Florida, and on travel days the Disney University staff took care of all logistical details. Bob continues, "We took care of their luggage, and we inspected every hotel room for cleanliness. Each night, next to the evening dessert plate, we placed reminders of any 'homework assignments' they needed to complete and a detailed overview of the activities for the following day. We were even careful about the placement of their luggage in their hotel room." Luggage wasn't simply left on the floor in the entryway; it was placed at the foot of each bed.

The Disney University team took great care in creating a memorable guest (trainee) experience. Taking it a step further, they arranged gifts from consumer products in the executives' rooms, including music CDs, DVDs of upcoming movies, and new marketing materials. This reinforced the value of surprising the guest and reminded attendees of the power of well-placed merchandise.

The Disney University team discussed key learning points with the participants after each and every one of these activities; the entire week was a living laboratory.

As the popularity of Disney Dimensions grew, senior executives presenting divisional overviews to the attendees started engaging them in solving actual business challenges. It was not uncommon to see a presenter use the program as a forum for problem resolution, challenging participants with the question, here is a problem we're having in my division. Does anyone have any suggestions?

Disney Dimensions and the Four Circumstances

Disney Dimensions captured the essence of a Van France–inspired educational event. It informed. It engaged. It was fun. It accomplished its business goals. This leadership program also enjoyed each of the Four Circumstances Van identified as crucial to the success of the Disney University:

- *Innovate.* The multiday, multivenue design exposed the participants to every area of the company. Until then, most executives hadn't ventured beyond their own area of expertise.

- *Support.* Disney Dimensions received the overt, enthusiastic support of top management; Michael Eisner and Frank Wells had a hand in choosing the participants and didn't hesitate to sing its praises. Dick Cook and Marty Sklar actively participated by giving presentations and engaging attendees during brainstorming sessions.

- *Educate.* Combining executive-level attendees from each operating division in the unique and interactive environment created a forum in which participants educated one another.

- *Entertain.* The Disney University team stayed true to Van's model. Every training event is an opportunity to be creative and interesting rather than the opposite: dull and academic.

The budget, staff, and time required to produce the exact equivalent of this kind of program could very well be beyond the reach of some organizations. However, the living laboratory experiential activities that led to advanced levels of cross-functional collaboration and creative problem solving are worthwhile goals for any organization. The price of admission to that sort of program is primarily an environment of trust.

The telephone call from Frank Wells confirmed everything the Disney University team had worked so hard to attain. Yet Carol is the first to point out that the program did not eliminate the silos. That was never the goal. In fact, to a certain extent, Frank and Michael wanted to maintain a sense of creative tension between operating units to foster a sense of competition. According to Carol, "We didn't design Disney Dimensions as a vehicle that would create one big happy family. In fact, we knew that a certain amount of tension would result in more creativity and better business results." As trainees and seminar participants, senior executives can be a cynical and challenging audience; creating compelling learning opportunities for groups at this level is a laudable challenge.

Dick Cook adds, "Designing an educational experience that will engage and motivate a group of senior Hollywood executives is a tough task. Why does Disney Dimensions work? It works because the Disney University and training at Disney is more than a series of programs. It is much bigger than 'everyone buys into it.' It is 'everyone *lives* it.' From my earliest days at Disneyland, I saw managers and senior company executives lead the way as role models. This creates a gigantic difference. They weren't above participating in training and leading by example."[7] Dick ensured that that message of involvement extended to the Disney Studio, where he supported and helped facilitate countless Disney University programs. He continues, "We all gave our time and energy to the Disney Dimensions program. We helped plan the agenda. We held participants accountable for the outcomes of the program and for participating."[8]

Virtually every definition of the term *university* has some version of the description "an institution of learning at the highest level." In his original proposal, Van France stated, "The Disney University should be a pioneering force, the world's first and foremost corporate institution for training."[9] Van included a leadership development component, arguing, "We need to develop leaders who have an overall understanding of the complex combination of skills and professions that have made the Disneyland show the world's greatest entertainment attraction."

Through the Disney Dimensions program, the Disney University team perpetuated Van's dream of providing more than new-hire orientation.

Beyond Orientation:
Executive Development

From Silos to Synergy

- The entrepreneurial and highly innovative culture created by Michael Eisner and Frank Wells at the Disney Studio had an unintended consequence: divisional and communication silos.

- Even a team of all-stars must communicate and collaborate.

- Lack of communication and collaboration between business units resulted in lost opportunities for merchandise sales.

Executive Development Van France Style

- Van France's model for employee training and development—entertain and educate—is effective at all organizational levels.

- Disney Dimensions engaged senior executives, reduced interdepartmental barriers, and created tangible business results.

Experiential Is More Powerful Than Theoretical

- The Green Light Experience, the Everyone Becomes an Imagineer exercise, and *The Little Mermaid* case study challenged the participants with real-time business issues.

- Visits to parks and resorts in California and Florida became laboratories for demonstrating and experiencing world-class customer service.

Applying Van's Four Circumstances

INNOVATE ● **SUPPORT** ● **EDUCATE** ● **ENTERTAIN**

Executive Development

How is executive development handled in your organization? How are Van's Four Circumstances used to reduce interdepartmental silos and improve collaboration and synergy?

From Silos to Synergy

- What is being done to fully engage executives in companywide collaboration? Who does it and how frequently?

- How could this strategy be improved?

- If it isn't being done, what is the excuse for inactivity?

Every Organization Is a Living Laboratory

- How are real-time business issues used in training and development programs?

- Are there examples of business hits and misses that can be transformed into case studies for executive development?

- Do executives in your organization openly assess business successes and failures? If not, what are the barriers?

Training, Credibility, and Trust

- How credible is your training staff and their educational material?

- How can leaders in your organization lend their support to training initiatives?

- What can your training staff do to create more openness and trust in its learning environments?

- In your organization, what needs to be done to promote and perpetuate executive development?

The Language of Success

Creating a Culture of Happiness

[Throughout my career], I had found that most people want to be involved in something greater than just being paid for a job. My basic story is about the two men laying bricks. When asked what he is doing, one man says, "I'm laying bricks." The other man performing the same task says, "I'm building a cathedral."[1]

—**Van France**

Disney University Conference Room, 1981

Van, sitting in a chair at the front of the room, has that familiar glint in his eye. His audience, with notepads in hand, is eager to learn. As the only speaker on the agenda, Van knows that his goal is clear: all the participants will leave this session understanding the magic of Disneyland.

His strategy is simple; after all, he always favors simplicity over complexity. Van will share his thoughts about the secrets behind one of the world's most famous destinations. Through this presentation, "The Spirit of Disneyland," Van will unveil to this new audience the most valuable secret: the Disney culture of putting people first.

A lot is on the line, and Van is determined to take this group far beyond polite nods of agreement; he wants an enthusiastic buy-in. The attendees are managers in the Japanese company that is financing, and will own, Disney's first international theme park, Tokyo Disneyland. Entrusted to carry the torch of Disney excellence to Japan, each manager is in the United States for an extended training and orientation program. Staying an average of six months, they are charged with learning as much as possible about operating a theme park, Disney style. Tokyo Disneyland is due to open in less than two years, and so time is of the essence.[2]

Despite the time pressure, Van wants these managers to grasp not just the ABCs of park operations but the true essence of what makes Disneyland great. His brief history lesson will be infused with values he learned from Walt Disney long before, values that have a proven track record of elevating the employee and guest experience.

Although Van has delivered various versions of this presentation countless times over the years, he still exudes youthful enthusiasm. The determination in his voice is as strong as it must have been decades earlier, the day he and his then assistant Dick Nunis unveiled the very first Disney orientation program to Roy Disney.

Rising from his chair, Van paces across the front of the room. Taking his time, he scans the audience, making direct eye contact with each participant. He begins the lecture.

"There must be quality in everything we do. It does not just apply to maintenance and construction."[3] He pauses long enough for his message to sink in, plus he has to give the interpreters enough time to convey his message to those in the audience in Japanese.

Continuing, he says, "Quality is essential in guest courtesy, in showmanship, and throughout our backstage activities as well as those on-stage."

Van follows this statement with his most important message, the one about creating a respectful environment:

"The initial Disneyland orientation program was designed to 'take the servility out of service-related jobs.' In the program, certain terms were coined which have been copied around the world.

"And, since hardly anyone except Walt Disney knew what Disneyland was going to be, we had to establish a sense of history by using the traditions of movies as a basis for functions at Disneyland."[4]

- "We don't have 'customers,' we have 'Guests.'"

- "We aren't 'employees,' we are 'Hosts,' 'Hostesses,' 'Cast Members.'"

- "We don't wear 'uniforms,' we wear 'Costumes.'"

- "We don't have 'crowds,' we have an 'Audience.'"[5]

"At Disneyland, I wanted people to feel they were involved in something more important than parking cars, serving food, or sweeping up popcorn, that they would be creating happiness for others."[6]

From Employee to Cast Member, Customer to Guest

Starting with the first Disneyland orientation program Van and Dick Nunis created in 1955, Van's message has remained the same: instill a sense of pride among employees about where they work and the jobs they perform. Van was determined to make Disneyland a place where customers and employees experienced second-to-none service. He knew that creating happiness would be impossible if employees didn't feel respected and good about what they were doing, regardless of their individual jobs.

One of Van's strategies involved creating a whole new language at Disneyland that would reinforce the dignity of every job in the park. Walt Disney originally set the tone when he introduced the concept for Disneyland: it wasn't an amusement park; it was a *theme park*.

Disneyland is a huge stage; Van leveraged this by introducing show-business terms. He reasoned that a new vocabulary, coupled with strong organizational values, could help bring pride and energy to the job. Plus, it wasn't limited to employees of the park; Van also changed the words used for customers. Thus, employees became *hosts, hostesses,* and *cast members*. Customers became *guests*, and crowd control became *guest control*. Over the years, the show-business vocabulary evolved along with the quality of the show. Ultimately, a core of powerful terms emerged from this approach that reflect the essence of Disney's sustained success:

- Good show/bad show

- On-stage/backstage

More important, these terms encompass values found throughout the company. Van and the Disney University pioneers were well aware of their task; creating a new organizational culture focusing on respect for customers and employees involves much more than the skillful use of a thesaurus.

More Than a Coat of Paint

Are the people who pay for goods and services *customers, patients, students, residents,* or *guests*?

Are the people working in an organization *associates, team members, partners, employees,* or *cast members*?

Merely changing nouns or verbs won't ensure world-class customer service or create a motivated and engaged workforce. Equally preposterous is the notion that simply slapping a fresh coat of paint on a dilapidated, run-down house will bring it up to code. Just as paint won't improve the structural integrity of a building, catchy words for customers and employees have no value without leadership support.

Yet the debate about how to best address customers and employees consumes valuable time, energy, and money in organizations that face more onerous issues. For those companies, assessing and clarifying organizational values is a precursor to future improvement.

A Culture of Actions and Words

Walt Disney researched his competitors well before building Disneyland and found that they all had one thing in common: their filthiness. From that point on, he let it be known that Disneyland, as well as the employees who worked there, would be a model of cleanliness. Walt's desire to keep Disneyland clean, insisting that "the streets be clean enough to eat off of," remains one of the fundamentals of its success and a cornerstone of the Disney culture.[7]

When the new-hire employees at Disney parks or resorts see managers and executives bending over to pick up trash, the message is clear: "what they taught us in the Disney University actually happens; I believe it." The values instilled by Walt and perpetuated by Van are reflected in the daily actions of cast members at every organizational level.

Ron Pogue's description of the terms *teamwork* and *show* indicates how words are brought to life: "Through our training efforts, both at the Disney University and in park operations, we instilled a sense of teamwork, constantly reinforcing our core beliefs of creating 'good show.' For example, supervisors and managers all pitch in when the park gets busy. On peak days, managers clear tables and install additional stanchions [poles] in the queue areas of the attractions to help create orderly guest control." When guest control is necessary during parades and special events, everyone helps. Cast members from foods and merchandise assist the operations team. Ron continues, "This makes all cast members feel part of a team with equal recognition and responsibility."[8]

Creating a culture in which actions and words convey the same message can also mean creating a culture of brutal honesty. Walt's and Van's message that pride, teamwork, and park cleanliness are indicators of organizational health extends to every Disney property, and there aren't any excuses for failing to attain the standard.

Jim Cora, retired chairman of Disneyland International, exudes the matter-of-fact bluntness that comes from decades of living in and promoting the Disney culture of teamwork, pride, and good show: "I recently received an e-mail message from a manager at Disneyland Paris. He was complaining that the custodians, before going on strike and just prior to the park opening that morning, dumped trash from the cans onto Main Street. I wrote back to the manager with the following question, 'Why were the trash cans full?'"[9]

Popcorn Empowerment

Picture the following scenario in front of "it's a small world":

> Timothy, a custodial cast member, is scurrying about sweeping up trash when he hears the child crying. Making his way through the guests converging on source of this commotion, Timothy sees the problem. A small boy, melting down in tears, is focused on the ground, stomping his feet in anger. The empty popcorn box and scattered kernels tell the story. Making matters worse is the boy's father, who is scolding him for his carelessness. This is definitely not The Happiest Place on Earth for the boy, his father, or the scores of guests watching the scene unfold.
>
> Within moments, Timothy appears next to the boy, kneels down, and says, "I'm sorry about your popcorn." Instantaneously, two things happen: Dad stops yelling, and the child, almost startled by the comment, nods his head and

stops wailing. Continuing, Timothy says, "Mickey Mouse told me he saw you drop your popcorn and knows you're really sad right now." After pausing for a moment to let this message sink in, Timothy continues, "And Mickey Mouse wants to know if you would like this big fresh box of popcorn."

Miraculously, a box of popcorn appears from behind Timothy's back.

Profound doesn't come close to describing the impact of this interaction on the child, his father, and the many guests who have gathered. Timothy is equally buoyed by the interaction.

Unfortunately, some organizations seem determined to undermine employee trust, morale, creativity, and effectiveness up and down the hierarchical chain of command with restrictive policies. Far too many organizations spend more time worrying about the cost of the popcorn than creating a culture that promotes staff unity and morale.

Handing out free stuff is certainly not the answer to every problem. An organization that constantly rectifies problems by doling out free goods and services (comping) is likely to be plagued by more fundamental issues. Even companies with the best products and tightest service standards must prepare for eventual customer complaints and requests. Too few are well prepared. "I'll have to ask my supervisor" reflects the sad state of organizational health for legions of employees and their disgruntled customers:

- Potential problems are not discussed.

- Resolution strategies are not considered.

- Employees aren't trusted.

The staff of the Disney University and the operations teams running the theme parks and resorts relentlessly consider potential problems and their resolution. "What do we do when operations don't go according to the script?" Cast members and their managers constantly assess and even role-play guest problems and resolution strategies. In the example above, Timothy undoubtedly mastered his approach well before calling it into play. His deft use of body language (kneeling down), the tone of his voice, and the strategic reference to Mickey Mouse instantly calmed the distressed child.

The cost to Disney of a box of popcorn is mere pennies, yet the message conveyed to guests and cast members is worth the weight of the popcorn in gold:

- *Actions speak louder than words.* "We really do care about your happiness."

- *Trust.* Empowered cast members can solve the most commonly occurring problems.

Popcorn empowerment embodies an organizational culture crafted carefully and methodically. Timothy's problem-solving strategy is only one example of good show on-stage.

Casting

The Disney strategy for creating good show and hospitality is a long process that begins well before a cast member ever comes into contact with the Disney University. In fact, the show for eventual cast members begins with the recruitment process, well before they are hired.[10]

How are the recruitment ads written? Do they reflect the company culture and the product, and are they informative? Where is the recruiting office? Is it in a prominent, well-designed building or in a basement somewhere?

The show continues with the employment process: applications and interviews. Thor Degelmann gives a specific example from his work in France: "Before the opening of Disneyland Paris we had to hire 12,000 people in six months. We wanted to ensure we could move a huge number of people through the system of recruitment and interviews in an orderly, efficient way that also reflected Walt's vision of friendliness, cleanliness, and good show. So we simply treated the recruitment office as if it were a major high-capacity attraction in one of our theme parks."[11] The Disney operating model—safety, courtesy, show, efficiency—works as well in an administrative environment as it does in a theme park.

Realizing that most of the applicants weren't likely to be familiar with the jobs performed in the unique theme-park work environment, the team came up with creative solutions. Thor continues: "We installed television screens showing videos of cast members performing the various jobs in our park. We decorated and themed the queue area, replicating a fun *Disney* environment." The recruiting team created an environment that entertained and educated at the same time.

Conducting first-round and second-round interviews on the same day eliminated the need for applicants to return multiple times for follow-up interviews. Creating a fun and efficient recruiting environment accurately reflected the work environment and culture of Disneyland Paris. It also promoted a process long espoused by Van France.

Despite Van's belief in the effectiveness of the Disney University programs, he knew the vital role of the hiring process in ensuring quality. Never one to mince words, Van stated, "Before wasting time and money on training and new-hire orientation we need to ensure we get the right people on board. Before hiring people, be clear about the job. Let interviewees know the 'realities of work.'"[12]

Putting People First

Unique verbiage, first-name-only name tags, whimsical costumes, and fanciful building facades mean nothing unless they all are built on a foundation of respect for people. One of Walt Disney's most famous quotes clarifies this value: "You can dream, create, design and build the most wonderful place in the world, but it requires people to make the dream a reality."[13]

Ron Miller, former president and CEO, offers a personal insight: "Walt cared a lot about connecting with and engaging people." Ron's unique relationship with Walt provided ample opportunities for embracing Walt's values firsthand. In addition to their years working together, Walt was Ron's father-in-law. Early in their marriage, Ron and Diane (Disney) lived with Walt and his wife, Lillian.

Ron continues: "I enjoyed reading the sports page during breakfast. I'd sit there with my nose buried in the paper while everyone else ate and talked. That frustrated Walt. Walt would start drumming his fingers on the table and say, 'How can you focus on the newspaper when there are people sitting at the same table?'"[14] The person-to-person connection that Walt encouraged at family breakfasts extended to his business style.

Ron and the popular child actor Kevin Corcoran worked together on the film *Old Yeller*, Ron as second assistant director and Kevin starring as one of the precocious children. During Kevin's career in the 1950s and 1960s, the film studios owned actors' contracts. This arrangement between the studios and actors, although no longer practiced, is similar to that in contemporary professional sports; teams own the contracts of their athletes for a specified period. Actors under contract could be involved in multiple films for a single studio. Thus, actors became an extension of the culture of that particular studio. Kevin, who appeared in many other Disney films, including *The Swiss Family Robinson* and *Pollyanna*, experienced directly Walt's dedication to family values.

> "My father passed away when I was nine years old and in the middle of shooting *The Shaggy Dog* film. I was devastated, couldn't remember my lines, and also had the pressure of my contract being up for renewal. Walt and the studio executives, well aware of my troubles, completely rearranged

the shooting schedule to accommodate my needs. Despite this, I was an emotional mess.

In those days at Disney Studio, we went to school on the film lot. One day, my teacher approached me at recess and told me Walt wanted to see me. So I ran up to Walt's office on the third floor of the Animation Building. Walt said to me, 'I'm sorry to hear about your father. I know how tough this must be for you.' Walt was comforting and went on to ask, 'Are you still having fun? Because if you're not, you don't have to do this any longer.' I told him I was struggling but that I would be fine if I had a little more time to get over my father's death.

I already had a good relationship with Walt; he often visited the sound stage and movie sets, plus I joined him during special events at Disneyland. Walt could read people, and he exhibited great empathy; I needed a velvet glove, not a steel hand, and he knew it. But what Walt next did inspired me then and inspires me now. I committed to getting the job done. Then Walt, in a businesslike but paternal manner, smiled, stuck out his hand, and said, "Man to man, let's shake on that."[15,16]

Kevin attributes much of his success both as a child actor and as an adult to the culture at the Disney Studio. Despite the success so early in his career, Kevin's life after acting has been devoid of the career meltdowns so frequently associated with those who attain childhood stardom. Although it was a nurturing environment, the studio staff kept the young actors grounded. Star mentality wasn't tolerated.

The Disney University reflects the same values Ron and Kevin describe. Van and his pioneering team created the vehicle by which to share with millions Walt's philosophy of providing an environment of respect and high quality. In an orientation handbook Van created for hosts and hostesses, Walt writes:

What you do here and how you act is very important to our en-
tire organization. [We have a] world-wide reputation for family
entertainment. Here at Disneyland, we meet our world public
on a person-to-person basis for the first time. Your every action
(and mine also) is a direct reflection of our entire organization.
So, it is vitally important to all of us to thoroughly understand
our responsibilities, particularly our responsibility for guest re-
lations and safety.[17]

Van's "The Spirit of Disneyland" presentation to the Japanese
leaders of Tokyo Disneyland was meant to ensure the culture that
Walt Disney had started in a small film studio in California would
thrive thousands of miles away.

The Language of Success:
Creating a Culture of Happiness

From Employee to Cast Member,
Customer to Guest

- Beginning with the original orientation, Van's goal always remained the same: instill a sense of pride among employees.

- Creating cathedral builders from bricklayers is a multistep transformation.

More Than a Coat of Paint

- The culture created by leadership support and mutual respect gives life to the fanciful words *cast member, guest, good show, costume, on-stage,* and *backstage.*

- "Everyone picks up trash" reflects the culture; no one is above pitching in and helping.

Popcorn Empowerment

- Cast members can solve the most commonly occurring problems.

- Cast members practice techniques for calming down upset guests.

Casting Office

- Creating a culture of good show among cast members starts during the recruitment and hiring process.

- Casting offices reflect the culture in which cast members will work: respectful, efficient, and fun.

- The safety, courtesy, show, efficiency model heavily influenced design of the Disneyland Paris casting office.

Applying Van's Four Circumstances

INNOVATE ● **SUPPORT** ● **EDUCATE** ● **ENTERTAIN**

Putting People First

What is the culture of your organization? How is respect conveyed to employees and customers? Do they know they are valued? How are Van's Four Circumstances used to communicate your culture?

Words Reflect Culture

- Does your organization use unique words to identify employees and customers?

- Does the culture of your organization support those words?

- How are organizational values reflected in words and actions?

- Which of these phrases does your organization rely on: *coats of new paint* or *foundation building*?

Popcorn Empowerment

- To what extent is problem solving a priority? How empowered are your employees?

- If empowerment is not a priority, why?

- Are your employees sufficiently trained and prepared to handle difficult customers and other challenges?

- Can the training be improved?

An Entire Process

- Casting offices at Disney expose applicants to a new culture. What message does your recruiting process convey to applicants?

- How might the recruiting process be improved (consider safety, courtesy, show, efficiency)?

Give Back

There is great comfort and inspiration in this feeling of close human relationships and its bearing on our mutual fortunes—a powerful force to overcome the "tough breaks" which are certain to come for most of us from time to time.[1]

—Walt Disney

Holding their prized creation, the 10 high school students slowly climb the stairs of the Disney Studio Animation Building. Their destination is on the third floor of this 1940s-era iconic structure. Soon they will meet Ron Miller, Walt Disney Productions' president and CEO.

As they absorb the environment, each step unveils more treasures. Original drawings and artwork from their favorite television shows and movies line the hallways: *Walt Disney's Wonderful World of Color, 101 Dalmatians,* and *Cinderella.* The animators' paintings of Pinocchio, so colorful and lifelike, seem ready to jump from the walls. When they saw the massive multiplane camera earlier on their tour, the students had an eye-opening lesson about the invention that brought depth and life to the animated classics.

Today marks the culmination of three months of intense work. Together, the students built a company, created a product, and learned a lot about themselves. This moment is like a graduation day, only better.

They are student leaders in the Junior Achievement (JA) program, an international organization devoted to preparing middle school and high school students to thrive in the global economy. For a full semester, each of them has devoted every afternoon to learning about the challenges of building a thriving business.

The Walt Disney Company (then Walt Disney Productions), through the Disney University, is sponsoring their school's JA program and providing their business coaches: one from the Disney Studio finance division and one from the Disney University. Still fresh on the students' minds are their many discussions with the two business advisors about production schedules, teamwork, fixed costs, and sales projections.

Approaching the office on the third floor, their host, the business coach from the Disney University, stops the group and says, "We're about to enter a special place not open to the public. Your dedication and hard work over the last three months are why you're here. Ron Miller, the president and CEO of Walt Disney Productions, has a few words to share with you about business, teamwork, and responsibility."

Milling about and barely paying attention, the students busily scan the walls and hallways for more unique artwork. The host's next comment stops them in their tracks: "You might be interested to know that Ron's office is the same one Walt Disney used for many years."

Order and attention restored, the host leads them into Walt's original office. For the next 10 minutes, the students meet with Ron. They explain to him the challenges they overcame manufacturing their product, and he shares with them lessons he's learned over the years.

As their time with Ron draws to a close, they make their presentation. It is a box containing their pride and joy, their JA product. Standing six feet, four inches tall, the former professional football player towers over the kids, yet his warm smile and kind words close the gap.

"This is the most interesting penholder I've ever seen!" Ron exclaims.

On a beautifully stained oak base stands a three-inch by four-inch piece of diamond-shaped clear glass. Etched into the glass is Donald Duck, doffing his famous sailor cap. The pen is mounted on the base, right next to Donald. Most impressive to Ron is the copyright symbol—©—that is etched into the lower corner of the glass. These kids have done their homework.

The meeting should have ended here, but Ron sees an opportunity with the copyright symbol and engages the students.

"How many of you know the name of the very first Disney cartoon character?"

"Mickey Mouse!" they all shout at once.

"That's a good guess," offers Ron. "Most people give the same answer, but it wasn't Mickey." Ron pauses and then adds, "Walt's first character was Oswald the Lucky Rabbit."

The students look at him in disbelief. Ron then shares with them a brief summary of the devastating story of Walt losing the ownership rights to Oswald in 1928. Oswald wasn't trademarked or copyrighted by Disney: Walt didn't *own* Oswald.

Ron uses this example to reinforce with the students the need to overcome challenges. He shares with them how Walt turned the Oswald tragedy into something magical. Instead of worrying about the past, Walt moved forward: he created Mickey Mouse.[2]

The ear-to-ear smiles on the students' faces broadcast a collective sense of pride and maturity unimaginable three months ago. The commitment to Junior Achievement is but one example of Disney's connection to community. The benefits to the students are many; the benefits to the company are equally valuable.

Connecting to Community

The value of being a good corporate citizen is undeniable. Giving back through corporate philanthropy comes in a variety of forms, whether through employee volunteerism or through donations of products or cash. Put simply, giving back to the communities in which a company operates creates multiple benefits:[3]

- Employees want to work for companies they admire and respect.

- Customers patronize and support organizations they respect.

- Volunteer activities help develop employee leadership and teamwork skills, building confidence and morale.

Through volunteerism and strategic philanthropy, an organization becomes a valued neighbor.

Walt Disney set an example of giving back throughout his career. One example is his support of the John Tracy Clinic, a leading diagnostic and education center for young children with hearing loss. Walt's involvement with the clinic, which was founded in 1942, came in a variety of ways. He served on the clinic's board of directors and actively participated in fund-raising activities. With rolled-up sleeves and wearing a cook's apron, Walt didn't hesitate to serve meals and clear plates during fund-raising events. Leveraging the strength of the studio, Walt also funded and provided support for *Listening Eyes,* a short film describing the clinic. [4, 5, 6]

Disney VoluntEARS, the renowned employee volunteer program, builds on Walt's legacy of giving back. Getting its start in the Disney University as the Community Action Program, Disney VoluntEARS supports multiple programs for helping children, protecting the environment, and supporting the arts. Through Disney VoluntEARS, cast members have given millions of hours of volunteer service in domestic and international markets.[7]

Jeff Hoffman, retired vice president of Disney Worldwide Outreach, spent most of his 30-year career developing and running Disney's community outreach initiatives. A veteran of the Disney University, he helped establish the Disney VoluntEARS program.

Why was it important to transfer Disney University concepts to Disney Worldwide Outreach initiatives? As Jeff explains "We infused into all of our programs the concepts of good show that Van France taught. We believed in giving our volunteers and our communities the same level of guest service we give our theme park and resort guests."

In addition to the millions of volunteer hours donated by cast members around the world, Disney VoluntEARS balances goodwill with good show. Jeff offers a humorous yet clear example of maintaining show as a volunteer: "Our best efforts could be undermined in an instant. After all, we can't have a volunteer wearing a Disney VoluntEARS T-shirt, holding a beer, and smoking a cigarette."[8]

Cast members engaged in community events efforts know well the value they provide. As representatives of the company, although they are technically off the clock, they fully embrace maintaining the Disney show regardless of locale.

Disney University and the
San Francisco Homeless

The two Disney University executives arrive in San Francisco for their meeting with the mayor, not quite sure what the day will bring. Highly competent in their roles as corporate trainers, both have years of experience dealing with rooms full of demanding leaders at the Walt Disney Studio.

Today is different. Despite their comfort in the business world, both experience the sensation that comes with unease: butterflies in the stomach. Could they bring a sense of the Disney Magic to San Francisco's homeless shelters? Seeking creative ways to address this major problem plaguing his city, the mayor reached out to Disney to seek advice.

At the meeting, the mayor explains the many challenges facing the city and then lays out his plans to improve the environment in homeless shelters both for the homeless and for the staff. The mayor's plan is ambitious and has merit; he is determined to increase the levels of quality, service, and respect in the shelters.

Inspired by a recent family vacation to Disneyland, the mayor is determined to re-create Disney's efficient and friendly environment.[9] Spending the day giving the Disney University executives a tour of the shelters, the mayor introduces to them the staff and many of the homeless in each shelter.

After the tour, the Disney University executives will meet with key staff members of the shelters and exchange ideas for improving service to the homeless.

One of the two executives, Carol Davis-Fernald, shares a vital message that ultimately drove many changes in the shelters: "We were very careful to point out we were aware of the distinct differences between Disneyland and a homeless shelter and that we weren't there to tell them how to do their jobs. But we did emphasize the power of treating visitors (whether they be patients, customers, clients or the homeless) like guests."[10]

The mayor, thrilled about the results of the meeting, provides examples of improvements in staff attitude, morale, and service in the shelters:

- *Be our guest.* "The Disney University managers reminded us of the elegance and value of treating the homeless as guests . . . making them feel welcomed."

- *Inspiration.* "The spirit of service and volunteerism displayed by the Disney University team inspired my staff. Disneyland is the best in the world at what they do, and we, as providers of services to our homeless population, can also be the best."

- *Facilities mirror feelings.* "We repainted and upgraded the furniture in our shelters and diagnostic centers. If we displayed pride in our environment, so would others."[11]

The Disney University team felt strongly that the culture of respect encouraged by the mayor was genuine. As Carol recalls, "Even before meeting them, I knew our discussion with the staff would live on. During our tour of the city the mayor proceeded to meet and greet by name every staff member and a good number of the homeless in each shelter."

Walking back to his office, the mayor further demonstrated his dedication. Just as Walt Disney and Van France had done by tirelessly walking the park at Disneyland, the mayor walked the city. He knew the front lines and wasn't above rolling up his sleeves and participating. As they ascended the stairs leading up to the city hall, the mayor bent down and picked up a piece of trash.[12]

Disney-style respect, friendliness, and efficiency have a place in any organization, and giving back has a long shelf-life.

Many years later, the mayor, Art Agnos, continues to express his appreciation: "I remember that visit very well because I have recounted the story in numerous presentations over the years. The Disney University staff was outstanding. Their message was on target, and the leadership at Disney Studio was terrific."[13] Although the Disney University team acted in a voluntary capacity, Mayor Agnos felt compelled to reciprocate. In gratitude, he presented to the Disney University team a memento unique to his city: a brass-plated rivet from the Golden Gate Bridge.

People want to work for and volunteer for organizations they admire and respect. Consumers, whether paying customers or recipients of social services, gravitate toward organizations that demonstrate good corporate citizenship. Strategic philanthropy builds brand equity and employee morale and is a vital component for differentiation in the marketplace.[14]

Volunteerism and strategic philanthropy activities reveal the true culture of an organization. Community involvement needn't be limited to a single activity or to donating money. Leaders must set the tone of giving back. The most effective demonstrate their commitment by getting out from behind a desk, rolling up their sleeves, and diving in. Giving back is much more than writing a check.

Give Back

Connecting to Community

- Volunteerism and strategic philanthropy activities reveal the true culture of an organization.

- Employees want to work for companies they admire and respect.

- Customers patronize and support organizations they respect.

- Volunteer activities help develop employee leadership and teamwork skills, building confidence and morale.

- Walt Disney set the tone for giving back throughout his career.

More Than Money Can Buy

- Giving back is much more than writing a check. It is clearing tables at charity events, mentoring/coaching students, and improving conditions for those less fortunate.

- The Disney VoluntEARS employee volunteer program builds on Walt's legacy of giving.

- Disney VoluntEARS maintain show when volunteering.

Applying Van's Four Circumstances

INNOVATE ● **SUPPORT** ● **EDUCATE** ● **ENTERTAIN**

Giving Back

Is volunteerism and strategic philanthropy part of the culture of your organization? How are Van's Four Circumstances used to help those in need?

Community Connections

- Do you have a corporate philanthropy program?

- How does your organization give back? Employee volunteerism? Donation of product? Cash donations?

- How could these programs be improved?

- How can your organization involve more employees?

- How can your organization expand to support more communities?

- Are employees informed about the impact of their philanthropic efforts?

More Than Money

- How engaged are your leaders in philanthropic activities?

- Do the leaders at your organization roll up their sleeves and participate?

- How could leadership involvement be improved?

Communicate Globally: Spanning the Gaps—Cultural, Linguistic, and Generational

We have to face the fact that we have some unique communications problems. Geography is one. Our complex combination of functions and talents is another.[1]

—Van France

Tokyo Disneyland's grand opening is a week away. Disney's first international theme park is poised to help launch the brand into a whole new era of global expansion. Years of detailed negotiations and numerous construction challenges are comfortably in the past, and it is finally time to unveil this gem to the world.

A series of well-orchestrated marketing and public relations campaigns have created tremendous curiosity about Tokyo Disneyland (TDL) throughout Japan and in the international community. But there is one more activity that must take place before opening the gates of TDL to the public: the press event.

No stranger to the world of show business and extravaganzas, the Disney team has decades of experience creating media events to promote new resorts, theme parks, and attractions in California and Florida. Members of the press representing major news and mass media organizations are invited into the park for a preview, the equivalent of an open house.

At TDL's invitation-only preview event, the media will be treated to tours of attractions, restaurants, and stores. As resort guests, they will get a long-awaited chance to sample the food, wander in and out of on-stage areas, and, most important, enjoy the attractions.

A press event is a massive, stress-inducing public dress rehearsal for thousands of cast members. Whether they are working on-stage or backstage, the countless details associated with an event of this magnitude challenge even the most seasoned teams of operations veterans. Yet for the most part, the TDL operations team consists of theme park rookies.

Indeed, a core group of Japanese managers and supervisors have received months of training from an elite group of Disneyland operations professionals. Many Japanese managers were transferred to the United States, spending months learning the details of running a theme park, Disney style; some even participated in the grand openings of attractions and theme parks in California and Florida. But as with any grand opening, there are endless details and many fingers in the pie, and some things simply fall through the cracks.

In preparation for the press event, the custodial and groundskeeping crews have been hard at work cleaning, polishing, and scrubbing every attraction, every restaurant, and every store. Flower beds are repeatedly checked for wilted or dying plants. Tokyo Disneyland is spotless and ready for the big day.

And this has created a huge problem.

Enthusiastically embracing the mission to "make the park shine," the custodial crew cleaned the Haunted Mansion. It isn't just prepped and readied for the big day; it is spotless! All the dust is gone. The spooky cobwebs have been removed. The Haunted Mansion is immaculate—it no longer looks HAUNTED.[2,3,4]

Ron Pogue, vice president of Disneyland International and Walt Disney Attractions, Japan, recalls, "The Japanese custodial crew wanted everything to look perfect for the press event, so they tidied up the old mansion."[5] Unfortunately, in their enthusiasm, the custodians managed to eliminate meticulously created and specifically placed artwork. They removed all the rubber cement cobwebs, wallpaper stains, and dust on the velvet curtains that had been purposely and carefully applied by a team of artists to make the place look haunted. The art of aging and graining, a process commonly used in the worlds of theater and film, involves the precise application of paint and other materials to on-stage props and buildings, creating a sense of realism. In the Haunted Mansion, artists spent weeks transforming the newly built mansion into an old, decrepit *haunted* mansion. In one night, the graveyard custodial crew transformed the aged and grained Haunted Mansion into a building so clean, shiny, and spotless, it could have passed the white-glove inspection of the strictest inspectors.

Steve Lewelling, the director of operations at Tokyo Disneyland, has a lasting memory of the incident. Living in Japan as part of the start-up team, Steve got a wake-up call—literally. "The call came at 2 a.m. My manager of custodial, another American expatriate, called me at home, woke me up, and said, 'Steve, they've cleaned the Haunted Mansion!' I couldn't believe this guy was calling me in the middle of the night simply to tell me the Japanese custodians had done their job." As the details started to emerge, Steve realized the gravity of the situation. What had taken the artists three weeks to create had gone down the drain. "We had just put the artists on a plane and sent them back to California," recalls Steve. "I was on the telephone scrambling to get them back, and their plane hadn't even landed in Los Angeles!"[6]

Although it was not "spooky" enough to open during the press event, the artists returned to Japan and miraculously readied the Haunted Mansion . . . again.

A Cultural Divide: How Clean Is Clean?

Tokyo Disneyland would be full of new challenges: construction on a landfill, design issues resulting from the weather, and then the hiring and training of 4,000 new cast members. Amplifying all of these challenges was the 5,000-mile and 16-hour time difference between California and Japan. Incredibly, all these challenges paled in comparison with the real challenge the leaders at Disneyland were facing: the cultural and linguistic differences between the two countries.

The custodians responsible for scrubbing clean the Haunted Mansion had many years of experience in their field; all were professionals. Collectively, they had decades of working in hospitals, factories, hotels, and office environments. And therein lay the problem. They knew how to clean those environments. A Haunted Mansion in a theme park is a decidedly different environment—a different culture—as is the process for its upkeep.

The cultures in which the custodians spent many years learning and honing their craft—hospitals, factories, and offices—had their standards of "clean" and specific procedures by which clean should be attained. The custodians, new to the world of show business, simply applied the standards from their previous places of employment in the new environment of the Haunted Mansion.

Unfortunately, a commonsense practice in one culture is not a guarantor of success in another; one size doesn't fit all. The preopening training for custodians at TDL, a quite extensive and detailed process, hadn't covered all the bases. And the problem wasn't strictly linguistic; an army of expert interpreters and translators bridged the language gap from the earliest days of the project and well beyond the grand opening. Manuals translated into Japanese detailed every operation. The problem wasn't custodial expertise; the problem plaguing the custodial team was a two-part challenge that affects many international and intercultural teams:

- *Assumptions were made.* Although the Japanese custodians were experts in their field, they had never maintained a building intentionally made to look filthy. The American trainers assumed that the custodians knew how to do the job and overlooked key details. Custodians, confident from their years of experience, assumed that this environment was no different from others.

- *Expectations weren't clear.* "Clean the building." How many times in the past had the custodians heard this directive? Clean is clean—that's common sense, correct? After all, this group of custodians had successfully cleaned many other attractions at TDL. Space Mountain was spotless, and their American trainers were thrilled! But the Haunted Mansion was different, and neither the Japanese nor the Americans clarified their expectations.

The collision of unspoken expectations and misguided assumptions magnifies opportunities for misunderstanding on teams whose members come from different cultures. Linguistic differences, often blamed as the primary source of misunderstanding, are simply the tip of the iceberg. If language is to blame, what explains the misunderstanding between the custodians and their trainers? After all, they had world-class interpreters at their beck and call.

The Cultural Iceberg

Effective, accurate communication is never easy to attain. Even those with similar backgrounds and values must constantly employ strategies to minimize misunderstandings and miscommunication.

Adding age, linguistic, cultural, and geographic differences to the communication puzzle further complicates an already challenging process.

The complexity of the communication transaction between people from different cultures is best described via analogy as the *cultural iceberg*. If language and communication style represent the tip of the iceberg (anything we can detect with our five senses), the portion below the waterline represents the values, beliefs, and common sense of those from that iceberg, or culture. Misunderstandings abound when those from different cultural icebergs come into contact, especially for extended periods.

As with real icebergs, the portions of cultural icebergs above and below the waterline are not balanced. The small tip of the iceberg gets a lot of attention when we interact with others—we focus on verbal and nonverbal messages—but the portion below the waterline deserves as much, if not more, attention. The below-the-waterline common sense and values of one culture can be disastrous if applied in another.

Understanding the whole iceberg is vital. The Haunted Mansion debacle could have been avoided if the American Tokyo Disneyland trainers and their newly hired custodians had taken the time to clarify what each group considered clean. In essence, both groups needed to put on scuba tanks and then dive into the water and take a look at the 80 to 90 percent of the iceberg most often ignored.

Operating from their background of working in hospitals and factories, the custodians had a vivid commonsense image of what constituted clean. The TDL trainers, with their decades of experience maintaining theme parks, had their own understanding of clean. Given their collective wealth of experience, the trainees and trainers thought they were on the same page: "Why, of course. Everyone knows that; it's common sense."

Cultures Are Neighborhoods

Groups, communities, and neighborhoods come in all forms, sizes, ages, ethnicities, and languages. Groups help us determine our beliefs, thoughts, and actions and distinguish between right and wrong. Also, every organization serves multiple neighborhoods. Even organizations operating exclusively within the boundaries of their own town, state, province, or country serve many neighborhoods and cultures. Those who choose to expand their understanding of the diversity of the neighborhoods they serve will thrive. Those who don't will be left behind.

A Disney theme park or resort is a small city, with multiple groups of professionals responsible for taking care of their portion of the show. As with any organization, those subgroups can become isolated from one another and gradually draw apart. Van France used the term *neighborhoods* to identify the diverse areas, functions, and cast members—the cultural icebergs—within Disneyland.

Van was well ahead of many other executives when he expressed concern about the obstacles he saw separating the Disney neighborhoods. These barriers between groups were creating silos, miscommunication, and distrust. Van, recognizing the value and creative power of a diverse team, worked tirelessly to remove the frustrations that can cause the icebergs to drift apart.

Exemplifying Van's concern for improving opportunities to integrate the needs of the many Disneyland neighborhoods are the following:

Job Functions

"As with any community, we have a variety of 'neighborhoods.' People in these neighborhoods frequently don't mix with others. Warehouse residents seldom visit the administration building unless it is on business."[7]

Our Age Range

"Although our community has been youth-oriented, the boy and girl 'next door' are growing up and now parenting their own boys and girls who also work for us. We have a wide age range which varies from 16 to 70. Our people reflect the maturing of the last 25 years. Some managers need to know, at least, that the people they supervise are different from what they were 10 years ago."[8]

Our Many Languages

"Although our community includes many who can speak most international languages, we also converse in technical jargon, which is difficult to understand if one is outside one's 'neighborhood.'"[9]

The "Disney Look" Grooming Policy

"Within the last 10 years, the 'girl next door' began wearing tooth braces . . . if her parents could afford it. But until two years ago we had a policy in our casting department that we would not hire anyone who wore such braces. This is, of course, totally ridiculous. But I wonder how many other obsolete policies are included in our policy manuals."[10] (Note: By the opening of Disney California Adventure in 2001, Disney's long-standing policy of no facial hair on hosts was amended to allow mustaches. Further amended in 2012, the policy now allows closely trimmed beards.[11])

Our Training Programs

"My opinion is that we need to alter the material we include in orientation. I may be wrong, but we need to reassess what is working and what isn't. Most certainly, a [newly hired] warehouse person must feel isolated if all the examples [Disney University trainers give] are about handling our guests instead of handling boxes."[12]

Discussing the need to continuously work toward bridging the gaps between the many neighborhoods at Disneyland, Van writes, "I continue to think of Disneyland as a community of people working to create happiness for others." Despite the thousands of cast members required to run such a complex community, Van argued against looking at them strictly as numbers on headcount reports and spreadsheets.

In a memo titled *People Behind the Numbers*, Van poses the question, "Why are the people behind the numbers important?" Then, in a tip of the hat to cultural sensitivity, he continues, "Is the person behind the number a college graduate, a landscape host, or someone who can't speak English?"[13,14] Dianna Stark, who began her 39-year career as a hostess on Main Street and on the Monorail, remembers Van as "a caring man with a big heart. He looked out for the hosts and hostesses on the front lines. He was also a huge proponent of getting more women into management well before it was in vogue."[15]

Van knew as well as any cultural anthropologist that sustainable and effective communication—across cultures, genders, generations, job functions, and economic classes—occurs when the members of different icebergs strive to better understand their own icebergs and those of their counterparts.

Cultural Flexibility

Appealing to multiple cultures and neighborhoods can be a confounding task for any leader and organization. Values and operating principles held in high regard in one culture may be challenged or even discounted by those in other cultures. Decision makers who are comfortable juggling multiple issues in a monocultural market can be baffled by the stream of new demands from the multicultural market. Blazing new territory isn't easy. One must consider:

- Where do we draw the line?

- When should we be flexible?

- These are our corporate values, and we must maintain them.

The line separating the various courses of action can be thin, and achieving success can be an exercise in trial and error.

Sake? Wine?

"We never allowed alcohol in our parks in California and Florida, and we stayed true to this philosophy in Japan." Jim Cora, in his role as Chairman of Disneyland International, recalls dealing with countless culturally driven issues. Disney executives, well aware of the historical significance of sake (Japanese rice wine) in Japanese culture, were determined to maintain the long-standing Disney value of an alcohol-free park. Flexibility wasn't an option.

Jim continues: "It was a real challenge, but we never gave in. Yes, we built a Japanese restaurant in our World Bazaar area, but we were determined sake would not be sold. It was a good decision. After the park opened, we actually received many letters from housewives praising our decision. They told us that since their husbands couldn't drink alcohol during their visit to Tokyo Disneyland, they stayed with the family the whole day; they didn't get drunk and lose interest."[16]

A decade later, the company took a different course at its second international theme park, Euro Disney (now called Disneyland Paris Resort). Facing a financial crisis and taking a drubbing in the French press for being culturally insensitive, Disney decided to part ways with the decades-old policy of no alcohol in the Magic Kingdom. Michael Eisner writes, "Marketing studies suggested that we'd sacrificed profits of as much as $11 million a year by not serving alcohol. As our financial troubles increased, we finally allowed beer and wine. It proved largely irrelevant, generating only a fraction of revenues that some had envisioned . . . the Europeans behaved just like Americans when they came to our parks. Rather than sitting down for extended mid-day meals, as they might back home in Rome, Paris or Madrid, they bought lunch on the run at our fast-food outlets, and mostly eschewed the beer and wine."[17]

Please Call Me Walt

The variety and nature of cultural clashes are endless, as are the solutions. Yet in the heat of the moment, some of the most obvious and simple solutions go unnoticed. The first-name-basis value of The Walt Disney Company is a case in point. Employee name tags sporting first names are now ubiquitous at businesses worldwide. This wasn't always so. Even in the United States, there was a time when the more formal titles Mr., Mrs., and Miss were widely used.

Walt, determined to create an environment of openness and creativity, was relentless in perpetuating the first-name-only culture. In 1955, hosts and hostesses at the newly built Disneyland had difficulty addressing Walt Disney as Walt. They felt uncomfortable addressing the founder in such a casual manner. Walt's standard reply to those who called him Mr. Disney was, "My dad is Mr. Disney. Call me Walt." This cultural value has deep roots.

Imagine, then, the intense "name tag negotiations" that occurred during the years immediately preceding the April 15, 1983, opening of Tokyo Disneyland. The Japanese, intent on maintaining their centuries-old tradition of addressing colleagues by last name, would have nothing to do with Disney's policy. Disney executives, equally resolute, weren't about to abandon a practice initiated by Walt. Corporate and national pride temporarily clouded the minds of the decision makers. What might now seem to be a trivial matter was at the time considered an insurmountable problem.

Once emotions subsided, cooler heads prevailed and a mutually acceptable solution blending the needs of both cultures was reached. The Japanese managers while on assignment in the United States had to wear name tags bearing a first name. It could be one's own name or even a nickname, but it had to be a first name. When in Japan, they could use their other name tags, the ones bearing their last names. Crisis avoided.

Don't Assume

Jim Cora, recalling decades of working with Van, cites a valuable lesson: "Van constantly reminded us, 'Don't assume they [new employees] know what we mean when we say, 'You're in *show* business.'"

Van France never stopped searching for bridges that would span the gaps between groups of differing neighborhoods and cultures. He never stopped in his efforts to simplify the complex and ensure mutual understanding. Although a prolific communicator, Van was well aware of the limitations of the written and spoken word. In his visionary report called *Disneyland: The Exciting New Era, 1980–2005*, Van cautions, "The terrible thing about the word 'communications' is that we usually don't know what we are talking about. What are we talking about?"[18]

The custodial crew at the Haunted Mansion knows exactly what Van is talking about.

Communicate Globally:
Spanning the Gaps—
Cultural, Linguistic, and Generational

How Clean Is Clean?

- The Haunted Mansion incident exemplifies a challenge facing every organization: overcoming cultural, linguistic, and generational gaps.

- As teams grow in diversity, so too does the importance of clarifying assumptions and expectations.

The Cultural Iceberg

- The complexity of the communication transaction between people from different cultures is best described via analogy as the cultural iceberg.

- Relying solely on one's common sense virtually guarantees failure in cross-cultural interactions.

Cultures Are Neighborhoods

- Van France used the term *neighborhoods* to identify the diverse areas, functions, and cast members—the cultural icebergs—within Disneyland.

- Van argued that those who choose to expand their understanding of the diversity of the neighborhoods they serve will thrive. Those who don't will be left behind.

Cultural Flexibility

- Appealing to multiple cultures and neighborhoods can be a confounding task for any leader and organization.

- Knowing when and where to draw the line between corporate values and cultural values is as much an art as a science. The different outcomes of not allowing sake in Tokyo Disneyland and allowing the sale of wine and beer in Euro Disney is an example.

- The Tokyo Disneyland name tag negotiations underscore the need to uncover creative solutions to culturally based problems.

- Altering the long-standing Disney Look grooming policy increased the pool of potential new cast members.

Applying Van's Four Circumstances

INNOVATE ● **SUPPORT** ● **EDUCATE** ● **ENTERTAIN**

Communicate Globally

How effectively does your organization communicate across cultural gaps? How are Van's Four Circumstances used to reach out to the cultures and neighborhoods you serve?

How Clean Is Clean?

- What is the equivalent of the Haunted Mansion incident in your organization?

- Have you identified the root cause of this incident?

- What strategies are in place to prevent a recurrence?

The Cultural Iceberg, Neighborhoods, and Training

- How many different neighborhoods does your training staff serve?

- Do training materials reflect the cultural needs of trainees?

- Does your training staff employ a variety of delivery methods to engage multiple cultures?

Cultural and Organizational Flexibility

- List examples of how your organization has adjusted to different cultures.

- Which policies are negotiable? Which aren't?

- What is your equivalent of altering the "Disney Look" policy?

- How has your organization benefitted (with employees or customers) as a result of the change?

Work Hard, Play Hard

The business we're in, if we can't have fun, how could we expect the public to have fun?[1]

—**Van France**

Stroke, stroke, stroke.

Sophie's lungs scream for air. Her arms, aching from the work, feel like two lead weights. Laughing to herself, she thinks, Why am I doing this? I got out of bed at 4 a.m.—voluntarily—to do this?

Sophie, intent on gripping the oar properly, barely hears the shouts of encouragement off in the distance.

"Go, go, go!"

Sweat pouring into her eyes, she grits her teeth and pushes on. The yelling gets louder as they pass the Mark Twain Riverboat.

"Don't give up!"

"You're almost there!"

The sudden splash of cold water hitting her face helps Sophie regain focus. "Don't hit the rocks!" screams a teammate. "Keep your heads down!" shouts another.

The peaks of Big Thunder Mountain Railroad disappear behind them. Sophie keeps pushing.

185

Stroke, stroke, stroke.

Skirting Tom Sawyer Island and closing in on the finish line, Sophie catches a glimpse of the Haunted Mansion off to her right. That sight, plus the cheering throng of fellow cast members crowding the deck of the Hungry Bear Restaurant, gives her and her teammates a much-needed burst of energy.

Then it was over.

"Great job, team Pain Street Paddlers. We made it!"

Sophie, gasping for air and laughing at the same time, scans the surrounding scene. Hundreds of cast members, screaming and cheering, line the shoreline of Rivers of America. Many are in matching costumes; the colorful aloha shirts, fanciful hats, and feather boas jump out at her. Some of the intensely competitive teams, (occasionally accused of recruiting "ringers") wear sleeveless muscle shirts and busily trash-talk one another. Sophie's favorite cast member costumes, however, are the T-shirts bearing unique team names:

"Canoe and Improved"
"Paddlin' Bayou"
"Last of the Rowhicans"
"Paddle You're Behind"
"Pier Pressure"
"Two Bit Oars"
"Candy Paddlers"
"Canoe Kids on the Block"
"Mouse-Ka Noes"
"Haulin' Oars"
"Disney UnivOARsity"

Adding to the fanfare is the cast member on the dock hamming it up Tinkerbell-style, wishing luck to each canoe with the wave of a magic wand.[2]

Amped up by this wondrous scene, Sophie forgets

about the pain in her arms. Exchanging hugs and fist bumps, Sophie and her fellow Pain Street Paddlers huddle together and cheer: "Next year, we'll rule the canoes!"

Over a two-week period every summer hundreds of Disney cast members descend on the Rivers of America well before sunrise to compete in the Cast Canoe Races. Lining up alongside the dock and spreading out along the shore, over 70 teams of 8 to 10 people eagerly await their turn to compete. The daily regimen of 4 a.m. alarm clocks, warm-up exercises, and multiple cups of coffee adds to the intensity and wackiness of the races.[3]

Each team gets a turn to load into one of Davey Crockett's Explorer Canoes and then race around Pirate's Lair on Tom Sawyer Island.

The fastest teams make the voyage in less than five minutes, qualifying for the more competitive rounds. Some teams never make it to the finish line. Unable to master the fine art of steering their massive canoes, they ram into the rocks lining the shore and are disqualified.[4]

Sophie and her team now belong to the unique club of tens of thousands of cast members who have participated in the Disneyland Canoe Races, a cast activities tradition at Disneyland since 1964. The cast at Walt Disney World created its own version in 1973: Canoe Races of the World (C.R.O.W.).[5,6] A former cast member explains: "The Cast Canoe Races fall right into one of those life events that qualify as 'you wonder why on earth you're doing it but wouldn't have missed it for the world.'"[7]

Cast Canoe Races are but one example of an organizational culture that values the stress-relieving benefits of play. The two departments responsible for organizing, promoting, and publicizing the races are Cast Activities and Cast Communications. Both have roots in the Disney University and bring life to Disney's long tradition of "work hard, play hard."

A History of Having Fun

Recalling his first visit to the Walt Disney Studio, Van described an intriguing scene: "Here [Disney Studio], wonder of wonders, were things which seemed incomprehensible to my industrialized brain. There were people playing ping-pong, volleyball, softball, and some just lying on the grass."[8]

In the early stages of his career at Disney, during the months before the grand opening of Disneyland, Van learned as much as he could about the culture of the company and its products. He wandered the halls of the Disney Studio, interacting with the executives as well as the animators. He took tours of the Disneyland construction site, gathering more information about this new venture from those handling the design and construction. Through this process, Van completed an exhaustive needs assessment before designing his first orientation program. His study of the company's culture, products, and operations taught him a valuable lesson: working hard and having fun go hand in hand.

Van Learns the Ropes

Van gained a deeper understanding of the Disney culture from a most unlikely source: the employee policies and procedures manual. At every other company at which he had worked, this document was dry and contract-like. What can be more sleep-inducing than a booklet full of rules and regulations about working hours, absenteeism, sick leave, personal phone use, and paychecks?

"At other times, in other places, my work was involved with industrial factories," Van said. "The structured environment of an aircraft plant, aluminum reduction plant, or an auto assembly line was totally different from what I found during this chapter of my work life."[9] Van got a glimpse of Disney's legacy of using humor to convey serious information when he read a 1943-era employee handbook, *The Ropes at Disney's*.[10]

A diminutive handbook at barely five by seven inches and 16 pages long at most, *The Ropes at Disney's* has a light and humorous design that manages to drive home important points while avoiding the stodginess so often associated with such material.

Illustrative of this is the clever cartoon on the page covering the serious topic of absenteeism. It depicts two employees, a man and a woman, scowling as they kick a wrench out the front entrance to the studio. The whimsically drawn wrench, brought to life with wide eyes and a startled expression, is the "monkey wrench." The message from this image is clear: that monkey wrench has no place at the studio. The accompanying text reinforces the cartoon and absenteeism policy: "We all know that unnecessary absence is a monkey wrench in production machinery. Consider that fact, and the short check on pay day, then change your mind about going fishing."[11]

A colorful drawing of a strand of bright red rope, starting on the cover and snaking through every cartoon-filled page in the handbook, leads the reader from one concept to the next. This powerful metaphor illustrates how each policy is connected to the next and the importance of everyone pulling together. After reading this employee handbook, a new employee had literally "learned the ropes."

Van's assessment of the Disney Studio culture revealed a core value: the vital role of humor and recreation in employee education, development, and morale. Procedures, rules, and policies, which are important to any organization, are more memorable when presented creatively.

Recreate and Communicate

Van didn't waste any time transferring the work hard, play hard culture of the studio to Disneyland. Shortly after Disneyland opened, Van formed the precursors to the departments now responsible for cast member recreation and communication.

The Disneyland Recreation Club (DRC) got its start organizing a bowling league, an art club, and the annual employee Christmas party. Over the years, the DRC grew into one of the best-known Disney University departments, Cast Activities.

The DRC and the later Cast Activities are famous for creating unique events by which to engage and motivate cast members. Perhaps the Cast Canoe Races owes its start to an equally off-beat employee event from an earlier time: the Parking Lot Olympics. Contests for the parking lot cast members included the following:

Cone stacking: stacking the most cones in five minutes

Cone laying: lining up the most cones in a straight line

The stress-relieving qualities of such "demanding" events proved invaluable to the participants. After all, these cast members are on the literal front line of Disneyland. Dodging speeding cars, answering guests' questions, and doing it all on a jet black surface in the intense summer heat take a toll.

Creating engaging employee events is one part of the puzzle. Spreading the word among cast members by promoting and then celebrating the activities is the other puzzle piece.

The first official Disneyland employee newsletter, the *Disneyland Recreation Club News*, debuted in November 1956. Although it was nothing more than a few pages of typed articles stapled together, the first paragraph of the lead story in the inaugural issue set the tone for decades of future publications:

The Ghouls Night Out
  On Sunday night, October 28, 1956, the Disneyland Hotel ballroom was invaded.
  The "invasion" of ghosts, goblins, ghouls and bathing beauties turned out to be the annual Disneyland Masquerade Ball.[12]

Years later, Van again turned to the written word as one of many tools by which to foster teamwork and improve cast members' morale. Creating and constantly maintaining Disney-style happiness is hard work, and gulfs between management and the front line started to emerge. In response, Van created another publication, *Backstage Disneyland,* as a way to, in his words, "spoof the problems in an employee publication and let employees know that we realized they existed."[13]

According to Jim Cora, Van helped bridge the gap by lampooning the problems. "Van started a little magazine called *Backstage Disneyland.* It was designed to be lighthearted and full of humor. The editor was a really funny cast member named Wally Boag. Wally, our vaudeville-style comedian, had a long and distinguished career at Disney as a stage actor. Involving cast members as contributing writers and artists ensured the authenticity of *Backstage Disneyland* and was a great motivator. One of those writers was a hilarious guy named Steve Martin, who has had quite a show business career after Disney. At the time, Steve was working in the Magic Shop."

The humor and honesty in the pages of *Backstage Disneyland* proved to be a powerful combination. Jim also notes that "Van knew the importance of communication as a vital management tool."[14]

Eventually, the *Disneyland Recreation Club News* evolved into a more polished periodical, *The Disneylander.* These two employee newsletters set the stage for Cast Communications publications still in use: *Disneyland Resort Line* and *Eyes and Ears of Walt Disney World.*

Through Cast Communications, projects that might not otherwise garner attention become morale builders. Offering a prime example, a former cast member says, "When our cast member barbershop was remodeled, we were all invited to participate in a renaming contest. Published in the *Disneyland Line* were hilarious suggestions such as 'The Hair Necessities' and 'Snippity Doo Dah.' The entries generated plenty of lighthearted debate."[15]

Deftly weaving humor into the written word is a fine art long employed by many at The Walt Disney Company. The roots of the *Disneyland Recreation Club News* and *Backstage Disneyland,* with their combination of informative and funny articles, run much deeper than those of *The Ropes at Disney's*, the employee handbook that so heavily influenced Van. Predating these publications is an untitled sketch of a man drawn by a teenage Walt Disney. Accompanying the sketch, dating back to 1917–1918, is the following maxim: "Develop your sense of humor and eventually it will develop you."[16]

The culture of having fun, which originated well before Disneyland was built, continues to flourish in multiple forms, and cast members thrive in the work hard, play hard environment.

Minnie's Moonlit Madness

Kris McNamara, who began her 30-year career as supervisor of Cast Activities and Cast Communications, recounts a vital lesson from Van: "Be creative, work as a team, and by all means, let the cast know you appreciate them."[17] The Cast Activities team includes in many of its events Walt's and Van's philosophy of educating while entertaining.

Over the years, cast members and their families have enjoyed unique events that energize, motivate, and in some cases literally shed light on park operations by answering questions such as the following:

- What does the inside of Space Mountain look like with the lights on?

- How are the fireflies at Pirates of the Caribbean created?

- What is the secret behind those dancing ghosts in the Haunted Mansion?

Whether through backstage and behind-the-scenes tours, annual parties, service awards banquets, sports leagues, or picnics, Cast Activities and Cast Communications create and publicize events that pull the cast together.

A good example is Minnie's Moonlit Madness. This after-hours event inside the park combines elements of a scavenger hunt and a trivia game. Over 300 teams of four people (one must be a current cast member) compete in a three-hour marathon of answering questions about Disney history, theme parks, television shows, and movies. Questions range from easy to difficult, and physical tasks add to the fun. Speed and accuracy are a must. Making it all the more demanding is the unique constraint placed on the teams: all four team members are tied together with a length of bungee cord. They must literally move together, operating as one unit.[18,19]

The challenges and questions carefully crafted each year by a team of cast members on the Cast Activities Advisory Board ensure that teams keep moving, exploring every corner of the park:

- How many horses are part of the carrousel?

- How many elephants are in the Dumbo attraction? (Hint: don't overlook elephants hidden in the decorations and posters that make up the entire attraction.)

- How many cannonballs and pairs of snowshoes are in Frontierland?

- What is the minimum height in feet and inches to ride the Matterhorn?

- Can you follow the clues to find the hidden treasure near Pirates of the Caribbean?

The trivia questions and brainteasers challenge even the most ardent Disney fans. The physical components of the evening can be equally engaging. Picture the enjoyable chaos of teams learning and then performing dance moves from a scene in the animated classic *The Jungle Book*.

The three-hour event concludes with team members enthusiastically comparing notes. Learning new and unusual facts about the company is always fun. Many use the evening to introduce their work environment to family and friends. Adding to their feeling of accomplishment is the collective sense of pride among the participants. Everyone knows his or her participation fee is donated to local charitable organizations; Minnie's Moonlit Madness is a noteworthy fund-raiser.

Through the vehicle of the Disney University, Van France replicated the enjoyable and productive environment he originally observed at the Disney Studio. Providing cast members with engaging and enjoyable opportunities for professional and personal development both inside and outside the classroom reaps tremendous rewards.

Ultimately operating independently of the Disney University, Cast Activities and Cast Communications continue dreaming up and promoting creative, off-beat events. Their goal is always the same: bring happiness to those who create happiness.

> Sophie and her fellow Pain Street Paddlers carefully navigate their canoe, gliding slowly next to the dock. Gathering their remaining strength, they now must get out of the canoe without capsizing it.
>
> In a reflective moment Sophie recalls her first day on the job, many months ago, when she attended orientation at the Disney University. Back then, just as the orientation program drew to a close, she pondered, How does Disney do it? How do they keep their employees so motivated and engaged?
>
> Sophie now knows the answer.

The Disney University and many generations of cast members tirelessly maintain Walt Disney's philosophy of having fun and remaining curious.

Why do we have to grow up? That's the real trouble with the world, too many people grow up. They forget. They don't remember what it's like to be twelve years old.[20]

—**Walt Disney**

Work Hard, Play Hard

A History of Having Fun

- Walt Disney's sense of humor and curiosity form the foundation of the work hard, play hard corporate culture.

- Even the most mundane document, a policies and procedures manual, comes to life in the form of *Learning the Ropes at Disney's*.

Recreate and Communicate

- Developing and promoting creative, off-beat events for cast members and their families, Cast Activities and Cast Communications serve vital roles; they bring happiness to those who create happiness.

- Minnie's Moonlit Madness exemplifies the philosophy of entertain to educate.

- Cast Canoe Races help energize cast members during a crucial time: the height of the tourist season.

- Parking Lot Olympics represents a daily task turned into a creative contest

- Employee newsletters direct attention to morale-building activities.

Applying Van's Four Circumstances

INNOVATE ● **SUPPORT** ● **EDUCATE** ● **ENTERTAIN**

Work Hard, Play Hard

How is work balanced with play in your organization? How are Van's Four Circumstances used to develop and promote employee recreation and communication?

A Sense of Humor

- What role does humor play in your organizational culture?

- Do your employee recreation events promote fun and respect?

- Can your employee communication tools (policy and procedure manuals) employ more creativity, artwork, and humor to ensure retention of concepts?

A Sense of Curiosity

- How do you encourage curiosity and teamwork?

- What is unique about your property, products, location, or operation that can be promoted with employees and their families?

- Can you create a learning and recreation event with components of Minnie's Moonlit Madness? If not, why?

Communicate

- Assess your current approach to employee communication and recreation. What message are you sending employees and their families?

- Do employees feel valued?

- How can you improve the speed and accuracy of employee communication?

- Does your organization have the equivalent of a Cast Activities Advisory Board to suggest ideas for employee events?

Epilogue

I was convinced that management and owners could come and go, but Walt's dream would last forever.[1]

—**Van France**

How do organizations remain relevant?

Organizational culture is dynamic, as are the conditions in which organizations must operate. The Walt Disney Company has seen its share of change, as has the Disney University.

From the earliest days of Disneyland in California and Walt Disney World in Florida to international operations in Japan, France, Hong Kong (and soon Shanghai), the Disney University has played a central role in perpetuating Walt Disney's goal of creating The Happiest Place on Earth.

Perfection isn't the goal. No organization can claim to have achieved or maintained perfection. The training and orientation programs Van France created in 1955 weren't perfect. The Disney University programs of the 1960s and 1970s look entirely different today. During its five-decade-plus run, the Disney University has dealt with numerous organizational, economic, and societal changes. Despite these challenges, the Disney University has adapted and continues to do so.

The Disney University is much more than classrooms, programs, and trainers. Like any employee development entity, it is a reflection of the health and welfare of the entire corporation. Any number of current and former Disney executives and cast members can compare the current state of the company, as well as the Disney University, with what it was "back then." As with any organization, there will be fans celebrating the past and those who consider the present state ideal.

Due to the immense popularity and reputation of Disney University programs, Disney Institute was launched in 1986. Their programs teach many of the Disney University concepts and strategies, further exposing the brilliance of Walt Disney and Van France to countless guests worldwide.

I hope that all the readers of this book will assess the health and welfare of their employee development activities. Whether they are directors of nonprofit organizations, small business owners, restaurant managers, volunteers, government workers, healthcare executives, or executives at The Walt Disney Company, there is always room for improvement.

Jack Lindquist, the former president of Disneyland and a leader who spent his share of time with Walt Disney and Van France, says this of Van, "Van was a maverick. He didn't fit into any box; he was his own box."[2]

The world could use a few more mavericks like Van France.

Notes

A Note from the Author

1. Van Arsdale France, Window on Main Street: 35 Years of Creating Happiness at Disneyland Park, Nashua, NH, Laughter Publications, Inc./Stabur Press, Inc., 1991, p. 4.
2. Interviews with Tom Eastman, retired corporate director, The Disney University, May 29, July 28, and August 8, 2012; interview with Kris McNamara, retired vice president, environmental policy, The Walt Disney Company, August 11, 2012.

Prologue

1. Van Arsdale France, *Window on Main Street: 35 Years of Creating Happiness at Disneyland Park*, Nashua, NH, Laughter Publications, Inc./Stabur Press, Inc., 1991, p. 10.
2. Interview with Dave Smith, chief archivist emeritus of The Walt Disney Archives, June 15, 2012.
3. Van Arsdale France, *Window on Main Street: 35 Years of Creating Happiness at Disneyland Park*, Nashua, NH, Laughter Publications, Inc./Stabur Press, Inc., 1991, p. 9.
4. Interviews with Jim Cora, retired chairman, Disneyland International, March 8, May 9, May 14, and July 26, 2012.
5. Interview: Dave Smith, Chief Archivist Emeritus of The Walt Disney Archives, June 15, 2012.

6. Interviews with Thor Degelmann, retired vice president of administration and human resources, Disneyland Paris Resort, May 7, June 14, 2012.
7. Interviews: Composite statement of all interviewees.

Pulling Back the Curtain:
The Orientation

1. *Gentlemen, This Is A Guest!* Training program for Disneyland managers. 1980–1981.
2. *Spirit of Disneyland* training program for Tokyo Disneyland managers. 1981–1983.
3. Disney Institute. *Leadership Excellence* Seminar. June 13, 2012.
4. Bob Thomas. *Walt Disney: An American Original*, Simon and Schuster, 1976, pp. 312–313.
5. Disney Institute. *Leadership Excellence* Seminar. June 13, 2012.

Lesson 1

1. Van Arsdale France, *Window on Main Street: 35 Years of Creating Happiness at Disneyland Park*, Nashua, NH, Laughter Publications, Inc./ Stabur Press, Inc., 1991, p. 71.
2. Interview with Dave Smith, chief archivist emeritus, The Walt Disney Archives. June 16, 2012. White Paper: *History of Disney Training.* By Dave Smith.
3. Van Arsdale France, *Window on Main Street: 35 Years of Creating Happiness at Disneyland Park*, Nashua, NH, Laughter Publications, Inc./ Stabur Press, Inc., 1991, p. 67.
4. Interviews with Jim Cora, retired chairman, Disneyland International, March 8, May 9, May 14, and July 26, 2012.
5. Van Arsdale France, *Window on Main Street: 35 Years of Creating Happiness at Disneyland Park*, Nashua, NH, Laughter Publications, Inc./ Stabur Press, Inc., 1991, p. 71.
6. Interviews with Thor Degelmann, retired vice president of administration and human resources, Disneyland Paris Resort, May 7 and June 14, 2012.
7. Interviews with Tom Eastman, retired corporate director, the Disney University, May 29 and July 28, 2012.
8. Van Arsdale France, *Window on Main Street: 35 Years of Creating Happiness at Disneyland Park*, Nashua, NH, Laughter Publications, Inc./ Stabur Press, Inc., 1991, p. 71.

9. Interviews with Thor Degelmann, retired vice president of administration and human resources, Disneyland Paris Resort, May 7 and June 14, 2012.

10. Interview with Bill Ross, senior vice president of public affairs, Walt Disney Parks and Resorts, May 10, 2012.

11. Interviews with Dianna Stark, retired operations training manager, Tokyo Disneyland, July 20, 25, and October 26, 2012; *Gentlemen, This Is A Guest!* Disneyland management training program.

12. Van Arsdale France, *Window on Main Street: 35 Years of Creating Happiness at Disneyland Park*, Nashua, NH, Laughter Publications, Inc./ Stabur Press, Inc., 1991, p. 71.

13. Interviews: composite statement of all interviewees.

14. Van Arsdale France, *Window on Main Street: 35 Years of Creating Happiness at Disneyland Park*, Nashua, NH, Laughter Publications, Inc./ Stabur Press, Inc., 1991, p. 71.

15. Fletcher Markle interview of Walt Disney, CBC, 1963.

16. Interview with Dave Smith, chief archivist emeritus, the Walt Disney Archives, June 16, 2012. Walt and Roy Disney helped found the California Institute of the Arts in 1961.

17. *Disneyland: The First Quarter Century*, Walt Disney Productions, 1979, p. 26

18. Van Arsdale France, *Window on Main Street: 35 Years of Creating Happiness at Disneyland Park*, Nashua, NH, Laughter Publications, Inc./ Stabur Press, Inc., 1991, p. 71.

19. *The Spirit of Disneyland*, program for Tokyo Disneyland managers, 1981–1983.

20. Interviews with Tom Eastman, retired corporate director, the Disney University, May 29 and July 28, 2012.

Lesson 2

1. *Gentlemen, This Is A Guest!* Disneyland management guest service program. Interviews with Dianna Stark, retired operations training manager, Tokyo Disneyland, July 20, 25, and October 26, 2012.

2. Interviews with Tom Eastman, retired corporate director, the Disney University, May 29 and July 28, 2012.

3. Interviews with Thor Degelmann, retired vice president of administration and human resources, Disneyland Paris Resort, May 7 and June 14, 2012.

4. Interviews with Ron Pogue, retired vice president, Disneyland International and Walt Disney Attractions, Japan, May 7, 9, and 14, 2012.

Lesson 3

1. *Spirit of Disneyland,* training program for Tokyo Disneyland managers, 1981–1983.
2. Interviews with Ron Dominguez, retired executive vice president, Walt Disney Attractions, June 14 and July 19, 2012.
3. Interviews with Ron Pogue, retired vice president, Disneyland International and Walt Disney Attractions, Japan, May 7, 9, and 14, 2012.
4. Van Arsdale France, *Window on Main Street: 35 Years of Creating Happiness at Disneyland Park*, Nashua, NH, Laughter Publications, Inc./ Stabur Press, Inc., 1991, p. 79.
5. Van Arsdale France, *Window on Main Street: 35 Years of Creating Happiness at Disneyland Park*, Nashua, NH, Laughter Publications, Inc./ Stabur Press, Inc., 1991, p. 16.
6. Interviews with Thor Degelmann, retired vice president of administration and human resources, Disneyland Paris Resort, May 7 and June 14, 2012.

Lesson 4

1. Van Arsdale France, *Window on Main Street: 35 Years of Creating Happiness at Disneyland Park*, Nashua, NH, Laughter Publications, Inc./ Stabur Press, Inc., 1991, p. 69.
2. Interviews with Ron Miller, retired CEO, Walt Disney Productions, July 17 and September 19, 2012.
3. *The Spirit of Disneyland* training program for Tokyo Disneyland managers, October 1981.
4. Interviews with Tom Eastman, retired corporate director, The Disney University, May 29 and July 28, 2012.
5. Interviews with Jim Cora, retired chairman, Disneyland International,. March 8, May 9, May 14, and July 26, 2012.
6. Interview with Darrell Metzger, retired director of Human Resources, Tokyo Disneyland, May 9 and May 27, 2012
7. Interview with Bill Ross, retired senior vice president of public affairs, Walt Disney Parks and Resorts, May 10, September 17, and October 13, 2012.
8. Interviews with Jim Cora, retired chairman, Disneyland International, March 8, May 9, May 14, and July 26, 2012.
9. Van Arsdale France, *Window on Main Street: 35 Years of Creating Happiness at Disneyland Park*, Nashua, NH, Laughter Publications, Inc./ Stabur Press, Inc., 1991, p. 69.

10. Interviews with Jim Cora, retired chairman, Disneyland International,. March 8, May 9, May 14, and July 26, 2012.

11. Van Arsdale France, *Window on Main Street: 35 Years of Creating Happiness at Disneyland Park*, Nashua, NH, Laughter Publications, Inc./ Stabur Press, Inc., 1991, p. 69.

12. Interview with Marty Sklar, retired vice chairman and principal creative executive of Walt Disney Imagineering (WDI), August 15, 2012.

Lesson 5

1. Van Arsdale France, *Window on Main Street: 35 Years of Creating Happiness at Disneyland Park*, Nashua, NH, Laughter Publications, Inc./ Stabur Press, Inc., 1991, p. 74.

2. Interviews with Jim Cora, retired chairman, Disneyland International, March 8, May 9, May 14, and July 26, 2012.

3. Van Arsdale France, *Window on Main Street: 35 Years of Creating Happiness at Disneyland Park*, Nashua, NH, Laughter Publications, Inc./ Stabur Press, Inc., 1991, p. 72.

4. Van Arsdale France, *Window on Main Street: 35 Years of Creating Happiness at Disneyland Park*, Nashua, NH, Laughter Publications, Inc./ Stabur Press, Inc., 1991, p. 75.

5. Interviews with Jim Cora, retired chairman, Disneyland International, March 8, May 9, May 14, and July 26, 2012.

6. Interviews with Jim Cora, retired chairman, Disneyland International, March 8, May 9, May 14, and July 26, 2012.

7. Van Arsdale France, *Window on Main Street: 35 Years of Creating Happiness at Disneyland Park*, Nashua, NH, Laughter Publications, Inc./ Stabur Press, Inc., 1991, p. 75.

8. Van Arsdale France, *Window on Main Street: 35 Years of Creating Happiness at Disneyland Park*, Nashua, NH, Laughter Publications, Inc./ Stabur Press, Inc., 1991, p. 72.

9. Interview. Dave Smith, chief archivist emeritus, Walt Disney Archives, June 16, 2012. White Paper: *History of Disney Training* by Dave Smith.

10. Interview with Dave Smith, chief archivist emeritus, Walt Disney Archives, June 16, 2012.

11. Interview with Dave Smith, chief archivist emeritus, Walt Disney Archives, June 16, 2012.

12. Van Arsdale France, *Window on Main Street: 35 Years of Creating Happiness at Disneyland Park*, Nashua, NH, Laughter Publications, Inc./ Stabur Press, Inc., 1991, p. 84.

13. Interview with Darrell Metzger, retired director of Human Resources, Tokyo Disneyland, May 9, 2012.

14. Interviews with Jim Cora, retired chairman, Disneyland International, March 8, May 9, May 14, and July 26, 2012.

Lesson 6

1. Van Arsdale France, *Window on Main Street: 35 Years of Creating Happiness at Disneyland Park*, Nashua, NH, Laughter Publications, Inc./ Stabur Press, Inc., 1991, p. 72.

2. Interviews with Carol Davis-Fernald, retired vice president, human resources and employee initiatives, The Walt Disney Company, June 16, June 24, and September 15, 2012.

3. Interviews with Bob De Nayer, retired director of human relations, Walt Disney Company, June 12, June 24, August 14, and September 16, 2012.

4. Interview with Dave Smith, chief archivist emeritus, Walt Disney Archives, June 16, 2012. White Paper: *History of Disney Training* by Dave Smith.

5. Van France, memo: *Reflections on Safety, Courtesy, Show, Capacity,* December 17, 1980.

6. Interview with Bob De Nayer, retired director of human relations, Walt Disney Company, June 12, June 24, August 14, and September 16, 2012.

7. Interviews with Bob De Nayer, retired director of human relations, Walt Disney Company, and Carol Davis-Fernald, retired vice president, human resources and employee initiatives, Walt Disney Company June 12, June 24, August 14, and September 16, 2012.

8. Interviews with Bob De Nayer, retired director of human relations, Walt Disney Company, and Carol Davis-Fernald, retired vice president, human resources and employee initiatives, The Walt Disney Company, June 12, June 24, August 14, and September 16, 2012.

9. Interviews with Tom Eastman, retired corporate director, the Disney University, May 29 and July 28, 2012.

10. Interviews with Thor Degelmann, retired vice president of administration and human resources, Disneyland Paris Resort, May 7 and June 14, 2012.

11. Interviews with Bill Ross, senior vice president of public affairs, Walt Disney Parks and Resorts, May 10, September 17, and October 13, 2012.

12. Interview with Steve Lewelling, retired vice president, Walt Disney International, November 1, 2012.
13. Interview with Craig Smith, retired director of operations, Disneyland Resort, June 12, 2012.

Lesson 7

1. Van Arsdale France, *Window on Main Street: 35 Years of Creating Happiness at Disneyland Park*, Nashua, NH, Laughter Publications, Inc./Stabur Press, Inc., 1991, p. 68.
2. Interviews with Tom Eastman, retired corporate director, the Disney University, May 29, July 28, and August 8, 2012.
3. Interviews with Tom Eastman, retired corporate director, the Disney University, May 29 and July 28, 2012.
4. *Walt Disney World: The First Decade,* Walt Disney Productions, 1982, p. 12.
5. Interviews with Thor Degelmann, retired vice president, administration and human resources, Disneyland Paris Resort, May 7 and June 14, 2012.
6. Interview with Jack Lindquist, retired president, Disneyland, August 27, 2012.
7. Interviews with Tom Eastman, retired corporate director, the Disney University, May 29 and July 28, 2012.
8. Interviews with Tom Eastman, retired corporate director, the Disney University, May 29 and July 28, 2012. Jim Cora, retired chairman, Disneyland International, March 8, May 9, May 14, and July 26, 2012. Thor Degelmann, retired vice president of administration and human resources, Disneyland Paris Resort, May 7 and June 14, 2012.
9. Interviews with Thor Degelmann, retired vice president of administration and human resources, Disneyland Paris Resort, May 7 and June 14, 2012.

Lesson 8

1. *Gentlemen, This Is a Guest!* Disneyland management guest service program.
2. Interviews with Bill Ross, senior vice president, public affairs, Walt Disney Parks and Resorts, May 10, September 17, and October 13, 2012.
3. Report: *Disneyland, The Exciting New Era, 1980–2005.* Van France, February 18, 1981.

4. *Gentlemen, This Is a Guest!* Disneyland management guest service program.

5. *Gentlemen, This Is a Guest!* Disneyland management guest service program.

6. Interviews with Ron Dominguez, retired executive vice president, Walt Disney Attractions, June 14 and July 19, 2012.

7. Interviews with Dianna Stark, retired operations training manager, Tokyo Disneyland, July 20, July 25, and October 26, 2012.

8. Van Arsdale France, *Window on Main Street: 35 Years of Creating Happiness at Disneyland Park*, Nashua, NH, Laughter Publications, Inc./ Stabur Press, Inc., 1991, p. 4.

9. Van Arsdale France, *Window on Main Street: 35 Years of Creating Happiness at Disneyland Park*, Nashua, NH, Laughter Publications, Inc./ Stabur Press, Inc., 1991, p. 75.

10. Interview with Dave Smith, chief archivist emeritus, Walt Disney Archives, June 16, 2012. White paper: *History of Disney Training* by Dave Smith.

11. Interviews with Bill Ross, senior vice president of public affairs, Walt Disney Parks and Resorts, September 17 and October 13, 2012.

12. Van France, white paper: *Disneyland: The Exciting New Era, 1980–2005*, February 18, 1981.

13. Interviews with Jim Cora, retired chairman, Disneyland International, March 8, May 9, May 14, and July 26, 2012.

Lesson 9

1. Interviews with Dianna Stark, retired operations training manager, Tokyo Disneyland, the Walt Disney Company, July 20, 25 and October 26, 2012. *Gentlemen, This Is a Guest!* Disneyland management training program.

2. Interviews with Carol Davis-Fernald, retired vice president, human resources and employee initiatives, The Walt Disney Company, June 16, June 24, and September 15, 2012.

3. Interviews with Bob De Nayer, retired director of human resources, The Walt Disney Company, June 12, August 14, and September 16, 2012.

4. Interview with Mike Vance, retired director, idea and people development, The Walt Disney Studios, October 2, 2012.

5. Interview with Dick Cook, retired chairman, The Walt Disney Studios, October 1, 2012.

6. Interview with Marty Sklar, retired vice chairman and principal creative executive, Walt Disney Imagineering (WDI), August 15, 2012.

7. Interview with Dick Cook, retired chairman, The Walt Disney Studios, October 1, 2012.
8. Interview with Dick Cook, retired chairman, The Walt Disney Studios, October 1, 2012.
9. Interview with Dave Smith, chief archivist emeritus, Walt Disney Archives, June 16, 2012.

Lesson 10

1. Van Arsdale France, *Window on Main Street: 35 Years of Creating Happiness at Disneyland Park*, Nashua, NH, Laughter Publications, Inc./Stabur Press, Inc., 1991, p. 21.
2. Interviews with Jim Cora, retired chairman, Disneyland International, March 8, May 9, May 14, and July 26, 2012.
3. Van France, *The Spirit of Disneyland* training program for Tokyo Disneyland managers, October 1981.
4. Van France memo, *An Essay on Traditions*. Interview with Bill Ross, Senior Vice President of Public Affairs, Walt Disney Parks and Resorts, October 13, 2012. Van France memo to Bill Ross, ca. 1984.
5. Van France, "The Spirit of Disneyland" training program for Tokyo Disneyland managers, October 1981.
6. Van Arsdale France, *Window on Main Street: 35 Years of Creating Happiness at Disneyland Park*, Nashua, NH, Laughter Publications, Inc./Stabur Press, Inc., 1991, p. 21.
7. Van Arsdale France, *Window on Main Street: 35 Years of Creating Happiness at Disneyland Park*, Nashua, NH, Laughter Publications, Inc./Stabur Press, Inc., 1991, p. 74.
8. Interviews with Ron Pogue, retired vice president, Disneyland International and Walt Disney Attractions, Japan, May 7, May 9, May 14, and October 23, 2012.
9. Interviews with Jim Cora, retired chairman, Disneyland International, March 8, May 9, May 14, and July 26, 2012.
10. Interviews with Tom Eastman, retired corporate director, the Disney University, May 29, July 28, and August 8, 2012.
11. Interviews with Thor Degelmann, retired vice president of administration and human resources, Disneyland Paris Resort, May 7 and June 14, 2012.
12. Interview with Bill Ross, senior vice president of public affairs, Walt Disney Parks and Resorts, October 13, 2012; Van France, August 29, 1985, memo to Bill Ross.

13. Display, Walt Disney Family Museum, 104 Montgomery Street, Presidio of San Francisco, CA 94129.
14. Interviews with Ron Miller, retired president and CEO, Walt Disney Productions, July 9 and September 19, 2012.
15. *Old Yeller* conversation with Ron Miller and actor Kevin Corcoran, Walt Disney Family Museum, 104 Montgomery Street, Presidio of San Francisco, CA 94129, September 22, 2012.
16. Interview with Kevin Corcoran, October 10, 2012.
17. Interview with Dave Smith, chief archivist emeritus, Walt Disney Archives, June 16, 2012; white paper: *History of Disney training* by Dave Smith.

Lesson 11

1. Dave Smith, *The Quotable Walt Disney,* New York: Disney Enterprises, Inc./Disney Editions, 2001, p. 107.
2. Author's personal experience.
3. Interviews with Jeff Hoffman, retired vice president, Disney Worldwide Outreach, The Walt Disney Company, July 23 and October 7, 2012.
4. *Old Yeller* conversation with Ron Miller and actor Kevin Corcoran. Display, The Walt Disney Family Museum, 104 Montgomery Street, Presidio of San Francisco, CA 94129, September 22, 2012.
5. The Walt Disney Company website: http://thewaltdisneycompany.com/citizenship/employee-engagement.
6. The John Tracy Clinic website: http://www.jtc.org.
7. Interviews with Jeff Hoffman, retired vice president, Disney Worldwide Outreach, The Walt Disney Company, July 23 and October 7, 2012.
8. Interviews with Jeff Hoffman, retired vice president, Disney Worldwide Outreach, The Walt Disney Company, July 23 and October 7, 2012.
9. Interview with Art Agnos, member, California State Legislature, 1976–1988, mayor, San Francisco, 1988–1992, September 6, 2012.
10. Interviews with Carol Davis-Fernald, retired vice president, human resources and employee initiatives, The Walt Disney Company, June 16, June 24, and September 15, 2012.
11. Interview with Art Agnos, former mayor, San Francisco, September 6, 2012.

12. Interviews with Bob De Nayer, retired director, human resources, The Walt Disney Company, June 12, August 14, and September 16, 2012.
13. Interview with Art Agnos, former mayor, San Francisco, September 6, 2012.
14. Interviews with Jeff Hoffman, retired vice president, Disney Worldwide Outreach, The Walt Disney Company, July 23 and October 7, 2012.

Lesson 12

1. Van France, white paper: *Disneyland: The Exciting New Era, 1980–2005,* February 18, 1981.
2. Interview with Steve Lewelling, retired vice president, Walt Disney International, November 1, 2012.
3. Interviews with Ron Pogue, retired vice president, Disneyland International and Walt Disney Attractions, Japan, May 7, May 9, May 14, and October 23, 2012.
4. Interviews with Dianna Stark, retired operations training manager, Tokyo Disneyland, July 20, July 25, and October 26, 2012.
5. Interviews with Ron Pogue, retired vice president, Disneyland International and Walt Disney Attractions, Japan, May 7, May 9, May 14, and October 23, 2012.
6. Interview with Steve Lewelling, retired vice president, Walt Disney International, November 1, 2012.
7. Van France, white paper: *Disneyland: The Exciting New Era, 1980–2005,* February 18, 1981.
8. Van France, white paper: *Disneyland: The Exciting New Era, 1980–2005,* February 18, 1981.
9. Van France, white paper: *Disneyland: The Exciting New Era, 1980–2005,* February 18, 1981.
10. Van France, white paper: *Disneyland: The Exciting New Era, 1980–2005,* February 18, 1981.
11. Interviews with Jim Cora, retired chairman, Disneyland International, March 8, May 9, May 14, and July 26, 2012.
12. Van France, white paper: *Disneyland: The Exciting New Era, 1980–2005,* February 18, 1981.
13. Van France, *People Behind the Numbers,* December 6, 1985.
14. Interviews with Bill Ross, senior vice president of public affairs, Walt Disney Parks and Resorts, May 10, September 17, and October 13, 2012.

15. Interviews with Dianna Stark, retired operations training manager, Tokyo Disneyland, July 20, July 25, and October 26, 2012.
16. Interviews with Jim Cora, retired chairman, Disneyland International, March 8, May 9, May 14, and July 26, 2012.
17. Michael D. Eisner, *Work in Progress: Risking Failure, Surviving Success,* with Tony Schwartz, Hyperion E Book, 2010, location 5338 of 8888.
18. Van France, white paper: *Disneyland: The Exciting New Era, 1980–2005,* February 18, 1981.

Lesson 13

1. Interview with Jack Lindquist, retired president of Disneyland, August 27, 2012.
2. Interview with Kris McNamara, retired vice president, environmental policy, The Walt Disney Company, August 11, 2012.
3. The Walt Disney Company, Chip & Company website, http://www.chipandco.com/2012/07/canoe-racers-disney-tradition-alive/.
4. Sarah Tully, "Around Disney: 45th Annual Canoe Races at Disneyland," *Orange County Register,* August 6, 2008.
5. Blog, Kathleen Prihoda, manager of media relations, Walt Disney World Resort: http://disneyparks.disney.go.com/blog/2010/07/cast-canoe-races-a-disney-tradition-of-paddles-up-before-dawn/.
6. Interview with Kris McNamara, retired corporate vice president, environmental policy, The Walt Disney Company, August 11, 2012.
7. Interview with Pam Miller, former cast activities representative, Mickey Mouse Activity Center, October 2, 2012.
8. Van Arsdale France, *Window on Main Street: 35 Years of Creating Happiness at Disneyland Park,* Nashua, NH, Laughter Publications, Inc./Stabur Press, Inc., 1991, p. 11.
9. Van Arsdale France, *Window on Main Street: 35 Years of Creating Happiness at Disneyland Park,* Nashua, NH, Laughter Publications, Inc./Stabur Press, Inc., 1991, p. 11.
10. Display, Walt Disney Family Museum, 104 Montgomery Street, Presidio of San Francisco, CA 94129.
11. Interview with Dave Smith, chief archivist emeritus, Walt Disney Archives, June 16, 2012; white paper: *History of Disney training* by Dave Smith.
12. Interview with Dave Smith, chief archivist emeritus, Walt Disney Archives, June 16, 2012; white paper: *History of Disney Training* by Dave Smith.

13. Van Arsdale France, *Window on Main Street: 35 Years of Creating Happiness at Disneyland Park*, Nashua, NH, Laughter Publications, Inc./ Stabur Press, Inc., 1991, p. 73.

14. Interviews with Jim Cora, retired chairman, Disneyland International, March 8, May 9, May 14, and July 26, 2012.

15. Interview with Pam (Miller) Lipp, former cast activities representative, Mickey Mouse Activity Center, October 2, 2012.

16. Display, Walt Disney Family Museum, 104 Montgomery Street, Presidio of San Francisco, CA 94129.

17. Interview with Kris McNamara, retired vice president, environmental policy, The Walt Disney Company, August 11, 2012.

18. Interview with Kris McNamara, retired vice president, environmental policy, The Walt Disney Company, August 11, 2012.

19. Eugene W. Fields, "Minnie's Moonlit Madness Tests Disney Knowledge," *Orange County Register*, September 14, 2011.

20. Dave Smith, *The Quotable Walt Disney*, New York: Disney Enterprises, Inc./Disney Editions, 2001, pp. 129, 136.

Epilogue

1. Van Arsdale France, *Window on Main Street: 35 Years of Creating Happiness at Disneyland Park*, Nashua, NH, Laughter Publications, Inc./ Stabur Press, Inc., 1991, p. 113.

2. Interview with Jack Lindquist, retired president, Disneyland, August 27, 2012.

Index